He Always Puts It to the Right

Phil King of Aston Villa scores the winning penalty against Inter Milan, UEFA Cup, September 1994 (Empics)

He Always Puts It to the Right

A Concise History of the Penalty Kick

Clark Miller

VICTOR GOLLANCZ
LONDON

First published in Great Britain 1998
by Victor Gollancz
An imprint of the Cassell Group
Wellington House, 125 Strand, London WC2R 0BB

A catalogue record for this book is
available from the British Library.

ISBN 0 575 06587 7

Designed and typeset by Production Line, Oxford
Printed in Great Britain by St Edmundsbury Press Ltd,
Bury St Edmunds, Suffolk

The section entitled 'Gary Lineker on Penalties', from
Striker: Skills and Tactics, by Gary Lineker with Tony Lynch,
is reproduced by kind permission of Stanley Paul,
an imprint of Random House UK Ltd.

98 99 10 9 8 7 6 5 4 3 2 1

Contents

Foreword

'Miller runs up . . . oh, I say, he's put it wide . . . well, would you believe it!' Thus might John Motson have commentated had he been present at Walton Comprehensive School, Stafford, in the autumn of 1975, to witness my first, and last, competitive penalty kick. The match was a Cup semi-final. The school first eleven was losing 1–0 but dominating the second half. Persistent pressure had resulted in a penalty. The problem was that no one wanted to take it.

I was a fifth former playing in the first team. I was a striker. I watched as the captain asked around for volunteers – no one offered. Then I found myself saying, 'I'll take it.' The captain looked at the coach, who nodded his head. That was it. The captain threw me the ball. Showtime.

As I placed the ball on the spot and walked back, I thought about the advice my father had given me on penalty-taking. My dad had played amateur football in Glasgow while studying to be a vet at Glasgow University. He had taught me to kick a ball from the moment I could walk. I broke my leg playing football with him at the age of three. (He nutmegged me, and I fell over trying to look through my legs to see where the ball had gone. One leg bent, the other stayed where it was and snapped. My mum was not amused.)

Dad was a fair player in his day. I still have a team photo of his, showing him next to Willie Omand and Ally MacLeod, who later managed Scotland. John Anderson, the referee in *Gladiators*, is also in the picture. Dad's advice then on penalties was to hit it low to a corner. Nowadays he's an advocate of the 'blast-the-hell-out-of-it' style.

I decided to put my shot to the keeper's right. As I turned round and ran forward there was complete silence. I side-footed the ball low and hard, just as my father had recommended. I remember feeling great as I watched the keeper dive the other way. A feeling that immediately changed as I saw the ball graze the outside of the post. I had missed. We lost 2–0. Heads dropped after the penalty and I was substituted. In the changing room afterwards no one spoke to me, not even the teacher. I went home without showering. I just gathered up my stuff and ran. I thought at the time they all hated me and blamed me for the defeat – the cocky fifth former who couldn't even hit the goal from 12 yards. I learnt later they didn't know what to say to me – they all felt guilty I'd been forced to take the penalty.

This memory came back with full force some ten years later. It was 1985, and I had become a solicitor in a big City law firm. I was playing for the firm in the Final of the London Legal League Cup, on the plastic pitch at QPR's Loftus Road ground. I was no longer a striker – a burgeoning waistline meant I now played at full-back. Despite the excess baggage, I still managed to score our equalizer – a bullet header from a corner. I suspect I looked such an unlikely candidate to score that the opposition forgot to mark me. There were no more goals, even after extra-time, and so the game went to penalties.

As one of the senior players, I should have taken a penalty, but I flatly refused. The memory of my school failure came flooding back and nothing anyone could say could persuade me to step forward. I bottled it and we lost.

I suspect lots of players could tell similar stories to these, particularly since the penalty is now such a vital part of the game because of the penalty shoot-out. Stuart Pearce of Nottingham Forest, Newcastle and England could certainly tell a similar story, although in his case it had a happy ending.

Pearce's penalty in the Euro '96 shoot-out against Spain was the catalyst for this book. The courage he showed in taking that penalty was, for me, one of those special sporting moments, and it started me thinking about the whole concept of the penalty kick. Whose idea was it in the first place? Who invented the penalty shoot-out? Who is the best penalty taker of all time? The best keeper? Courtesy of David Barber at the FA, I did some basic research and, months later, here we are. A journey from the birth of the penalty kick over a hundred years ago, to the present day, with a fair few stops along the way.

However, before going any further you have to answer two questions. There are no prizes and the answers are in Chapter 1 (so no cheating):

1. What was the nationality of the man who invented the penalty kick? Was he:
    - English
    - Scottish
    - Irish
    - Welsh

2. What position did he play? Was he a:
    - Striker
    - Goalkeeper
    - Defender
    - Midfield player

Enjoy.

Clark Miller
London, 1997

1 – The Good Old Days

Nowadays, it is popular to think of the modern football player as some sort of cynical, yobbish robot when compared with the paragons of virtue and individuality of yesteryear. In the 'good old days' players were more skilful and better behaved. There were no betting scams, sex scandals or professional fouls. Doesn't nostalgia have a wonderful way of accentuating the positive?

The reality is somewhat different. The fact is, there have always been badly behaved players, many modern players are just as talented as their 'good old days' counterparts, if not more so, and there have been problems with gambling and football since the start of the modern game, just as there have been crowd disasters, rigged results and sex scandals. More importantly for present purposes, we need to understand that the 'professional' foul is not a modern phenomenon. It was 'alive and kicking', or rather, 'alive and punching', even before the first player was paid for playing football.

The penalty kick's journey begins in the 1880s, a period of exponential development for the game of Association Football. Crowds were growing, play was much more competitive and, horror of horrors, players were beginning to be paid. There was now big money to be won, not just fame and glory and, just as now, certain players were willing to do almost anything to win a game.

Death in the Afternoon

The Laws of the Game, as they stood at the beginning of the 1880s, did not really carry much fear for the Victorian professional fouler. The game was pretty brutal anyway, as the following two incidents amply demonstrate.

On 19 March 1878, William Bradshaw was indicted at the Leicester Spring Assizes (a criminal court) for the manslaughter of one Herbert Dockerty during a football game held on 28 February 1878. The match was a local derby between Ashby de la Zouch and Coalville. Dockerty, an attacker for Coalville, dribbled the ball past Bradshaw who, according to the prosecution evidence, then 'jumped in the air and struck him in the stomach with his knee'. The defence claimed the 'charge' had been simultaneous with Dockerty kicking the ball past Bradshaw, although a number of the defence witnesses did concede that 'charging by jumping with the knee protruding was unfair'. The umpires (yes, this is still football, I'll explain in a moment), unsurprisingly, disagreed as to what happened. The Coalville umpire said the charge was unfair, his counterpart said he had seen nothing untoward in it. The debate was academic to poor Herbert – he died the next day of a ruptured intestine.

Lord Justice Bramwell reviewed the evidence for the jury and came up with the masterly understatement that there was 'no doubt that the game was, in any circumstances, a rough one'. However, he was unwilling to decry the 'manly sports of this country, all of which were no doubt attended with more or less danger'. The jury found Bradshaw not guilty.

Contrast the verdict in the Bradshaw case with the case of Henry Moore in 1898. Again the trial involved Leicestershire teams and was also heard at the Leicester Assizes (Leicester was clearly a tough place in the late 1800s). The report of the case reads as follows:

> Henry Moore was indicted for the manslaughter of John Briggs. The deceased was killed in a football match and the strange feature of the case was that a young man called Veasey, who was playing in the same match, and who had given evidence against the prisoner before the magistrates, was himself killed a few days later in another football match.
>
> Evidence showed that in a match between Aylestone and Enderby, the prisoner was playing back for Enderby and the deceased was playing forward for Aylestone. The ball had been passed to Briggs and he dribbled it past Moore, who ran after him. Briggs kicked the ball rather hard towards the goal and the goalkeeper ran forward to kick the ball and save his goal. Just as he kicked, Moore jumped with his knees up against Briggs' back and threw him violently forward against the knees of the goalkeeper. Briggs fell, Moore did not, and Briggs was helped off the field. He died a few days later from serious internal injuries.

The judge instructed the jury that they had to decide whether Moore had used illegal violence, and this time the jury came up with a guilty verdict.

Football in the early days was clearly not a game for the faint of heart – going down to the park for a kick-around was potentially a matter of life or death. The list of fouls for which a free-kick could be given was short, and, crucially, a goal could not be scored direct from any free-kick. The biggest problem, however, was not violent or dangerous play, but deliberate handball by an outfield player which prevented a goal being scored. At this stage in football's development, the authorities seem to have been more interested in stamping out something considered to be far more reprehensible – that crime of crimes, 'ungentlemanly conduct'. 'Charging', on the other hand (even if players occasionally were maimed or killed), was honourable and manly. Deliberately handling the ball to prevent a goal being scored was much, much worse: it was bad form.

Professional Fouls, Umpires and Referees

The Football Association's first legislative attempt at dealing with the professional foul was a resounding failure. In the early 1880s, the FA introduced a law which gave the umpires and referee the discretion to award a goal when the ball had been handled by a player other than the goalkeeper and, in their opinion, this had, 'prevented a goal being scored'.

Imagine the carnage such a law would cause today. Well, in the early 1880s some goals didn't even have solid crossbars. Initially, bars were made out of tape – solid crossbars did not become mandatory until 1883. Sometimes a goal would be awarded, or not, as a result of the wind blowing the tape up and down. Even worse, the crowd was often very close to the touchline and, just as now, the fans were no friends of the match officials, viewing them as interfering busybodies who kept stopping the game for no reason.

In the very early days of Association Football, match officials were not required. Players were gentlemen, and any dispute would be settled by the two captains. The real sanction against foul play came from the players themselves. If you could not behave like a gentleman then the other players simply didn't ask you to play again.

However, by the introduction of competitive football, in the form of the FA Cup in 1871, this system had evolved so that each side appointed an 'umpire'. Carrying sticks and patrolling one half each, these gentlemen gave rulings on the Laws only when appealed to by the players. The umpires were given the power to award an indirect free-kick for handball in 1873 and for other offences in 1874. They were also given the power to dismiss players, but only for persistent infringement of the rules.

This 'two-umpire' system was not unlike the proposal currently being championed by Arsene Wenger, and others, for a referee in each half of the field. However, the referee of 1871 initially looked much more like a modern referee's assistant than a referee. The ref was appointed by mutual agreement, stood on the touchline (or outside what was thought to be the main playing area in the event that there was no actual touch-line), his job being to 'keep a record of the game and act as timekeeper'. By 1880 he was arbitrating between the two umpires in the event they could not agree, and also had the power to caution players for ungentlemanly conduct, without consulting the umpires, although the umpires had to be present when the caution was administered. If a player continued to foul then the referee had the power to send him off and report him 'even if the player proffers an apology'. The referee only took over complete control of the game at the same time as – and as part of the re-organization caused by – the introduction of the penalty kick.

It was against this background – from the side of the pitch and thus among the crowd – that referees were expected to make split-second decisions as to whether or not the ball was going in the goal. Nevertheless, in the first year of the new law, the officials appear to have welcomed the challenge, awarding discretionary goals freely. However, as the decade progressed, hostility to this rule, and to referees, increased. It was a brave referee who exercised his discretion, particularly against the home side, and few did. As the marvellous book *Association Football and the Men Who Made It* later recorded: 'The attempt made previously to achieve this desirable object by giving the referee the power to allow a goal that had been saved by unfair means had not proved successful. It was found that referees shrunk both from the odium and the ordeal of making presents of goals to visiting teams in the sight and sound and within touch of a hostile local following.'

The professional foul crisis came to a head during an FA Cup quarter-final between Stoke City and Notts County, held at Trent Bridge on 14 February 1891. Just before the end of the game, with County winning 1–0, the County back, Hendry, fisted the ball clear with his goalkeeper, Toome, well beaten and with the ball clearly destined for the goal. Stoke were awarded a free-kick virtually on the goal-line from which, under the existing laws, they could not score direct. The County keeper and defenders stood directly in front of the ball and blocked the ensuing shot. The ball was cleared and Notts County won the match, going on to the Final, where some justice was done in that they were beaten 3–1 by Blackburn Rovers.

Clearly, action was needed. The credibility of the game was at stake. In June 1891, the authorities finally did something about it. Sadly, for Stoke City, a penalty-kick law had, in fact, been proposed a year earlier only to be rejected. The idea had originated in Ireland and, believe it or not, it was the brain-child of a goalkeeper.

William McCrum

William McCrum was a wealthy linen manufacturer, raconteur, cricketer and the goalkeeper for Milford Everton, a small club in County Armagh, which played in the inaugural season of the Irish Championship in 1890–91. History does not tell how good a keeper McCrum was, but he was certainly kept busy that first Irish League season. Milford Everton finished bottom of the League with no points, a record of 10 goals scored, 62 conceded, and were promptly relegated.

McCrum may not have been one of the world's greatest goalkeepers, but he was a gentleman and justly proud of his reputation for good sportsmanship. His obituary, in 1932, paints a picture of a man of honour who, in the late 1880s, was frustrated and angry at the 'win-at-all-costs' attitude that was now poisoning his beloved football. He had first-hand knowledge of the problem from his own playing experiences, and believed that anyone who failed to abide by the spirit of the game should face a sanction that would punish not just the individual offender but his whole team. I suspect there were many others who had reached a similar conclusion, but McCrum was in a position to do something about it, holding an influential position in the Irish Football Association. In 1890 he submitted to the Association his proposal for 'a penalty kick'.

The penalty kick may have been McCrum's original idea, but the person who 'put the ball in the net' was his colleague at the Irish Association, Jack Reid. As general secretary of the Association, Reid represented Ireland at the annual meetings of the International Football Association Board ('International Board'), which had been founded in 1886 to supervise the Laws of the Game. Reid formally submitted McCrum's proposal to the International Board for consideration and, he hoped, incorporation into the Laws, at the board meeting to be held on 2 June 1890. It immediately ran into a storm of protest.

The reception that greeted McCrum's idea was ferocious. Press, administrators and players publicly derided the idea. The 'Irishman's motion', as they called it, was a slur on the integrity of football players everywhere. As it was later observed in the press: 'Its introduction has been made the text for a vast number of sermons upon the evil tendencies of professional football.'

Some commentators even nicknamed the proposal the 'death penalty', implying it would be the death of the game as they knew it. Many people did not want to introduce a rule which effectively conceded that teams and players often resorted to unsporting methods.

This outburst of righteous indignation seems bizarre today. If 'professional fouls' were being committed, and just about everyone knew it, why bury your head in the sand? However, in 1890 this attitude was perfectly understandable. Amateur players, in particular, bitterly resented the attack on their integrity implicit in the proposed new law. When the law was eventually introduced they refused to accept it. 'Gentlemen' did not commit fouls of the type the 'Irishman's motion' sought to punish.

It was in such an atmosphere that the Irish delegation attended the International Board meeting, the penalty-kick idea in their briefcase. It wasn't even discussed. The June 1890 minutes simply note that the Irish Association had withdrawn its proposal. However, it had not been rejected, and the International Board had agreed to discuss the issue at their next meeting. The Irish delegation appear to have executed a rather neat tactical withdrawal, keeping their powder dry for the next battle. It was not long in coming.

At a meeting of the FA Council held in London on 21 January 1891, the Council again approved the Irish proposal and recommended it to the International Board. It had not changed, and read as follows:

> If any player shall intentionally trip or hold an opposing player, or deliberately handle the ball within 12 yards from his own goal-line, the referee shall, on appeal, award the opposing side a penalty kick, to be taken from any point 12 yards from the goal-line, under the following conditions:
>
> All players, with the exception of the player taking the penalty kick and the goalkeeper, shall stand behind the ball and at least six yards from it; the ball shall be in play when the kick is taken. A goal may be scored from a penalty kick.

The Notts County–Stoke City match had already taken place by the time the International Board met at 6 p.m. on

2 June 1891 in the Alexandra Hotel, Bath Street, Glasgow. The meeting was chaired by the president of the Scottish Association, G. Snedden. The press were excluded.

Reid was again the only representative from Ireland, but this time he was not the only voice in support of the penalty proposal. There had been a clear change of heart at the English Football Association, no doubt prompted in part by the Notts County game. Reid's proposal was seconded by Mr Crump, one of the two English representatives, and the new law was passed, subject to the following changes to the original proposal made 'after considerable discussion' (the changes are in italics): '. . . All players, with the exception of the player taking the penalty kick and the opposing goalkeeper (*who shall not advance more than six yards from the goal-line*) shall stand *at least six yards behind the ball.* The ball shall be in play when the kick is taken, and a goal may be scored from the penalty kick.'

The penalty kick was born!

A First Stab

This first attempt at a penalty law deserves close examination:

The first thing to hit you is the limited number of offences for which a penalty kick could be awarded: 'tripping', 'holding' or 'deliberate handball'. Amazing though it may seem, under the first penalty law it was still perfectly acceptable to push, strike, charge or kick your opponent. Well, at least you wouldn't get a penalty awarded against you. The limited scope was further evidence that the authorities were intent on stamping out those fouls which were considered to be 'ungentlemanly'.

Perhaps even more extraordinary to modern-day players and fans is the concept of the penalty area stretching right across the pitch. If you committed a foul anywhere within 12 yards of your own goal-line a penalty could be given. So, handle the ball near the corner flag, trip or hold someone on the touchline, and you could give away a penalty!

You also had to ask if you wanted a penalty – the referee could not award one just because he believed an offence had been committed.

And even more bizarre, the attacking team could opt to take the penalty from any point 12 yards from the goal – the definitive penalty spot was not introduced until the 1902–03 season. I have not, however, discovered any examples of players taking advantage of this flexibility.

Initially, the ball was in play again as soon as the kick was taken. Nowadays, the ball has to be touched by another player before the penalty taker can play it again, but not in 1891. If the shot hit the post and rebounded to the penalty taker, he was perfectly entitled to have another shot. If he scuffed his shot he could shoot again, assuming he got to the ball first. Some of you may recall the Charity Shield match between Manchester United and Chelsea in August 1997. Teddy Sheringham took a penalty for Man United and hit the post, with the ball rebounding straight back to him. In 1891 he would have been entitled to score from the rebound.

And today, if a penalty is awarded right at the end of a game, the modern laws allow the game to be extended in order for the kick to be taken. The first penalty law was silent on this point.

Finally, the 1890s player would have been mightily relieved to know that a goal could be scored from a penalty. What the rule makers had in mind when they drafted this part of the new law is beyond me. Presumably they thought they had to spell out the fact that you could score from a penalty kick lest some Smart Alec lawyer-type objected: 'I say, old chap, there is nothing in the rules to say you can actually score from a penalty, you know.'

The new law came into force immediately and was not a

huge success. As we have seen, there were obvious flaws in the first draft, and players – particularly goalkeepers – were quick to take advantage. These flaws, and the succession of law changes introduced to correct them, are discussed in detail in Chapter 2. However, a certain group of players had a much more fundamental problem with the new law. They refused to recognize it at all!

Gentlemen

In the late 1800s and early 1900s, the Corinthians were the best amateur team in England. Many people considered them the best team, amateur or professional. They held a special place in the public's affection and were comprised entirely of that creature the British public still hold so dear – the gifted amateur. A scratch team, of no fixed abode and comprising only ex-public schoolboys and 'Varsity' graduates, they were very good, and not just at soccer. The Corinthians could beat the best teams in Great Britain and abroad at football, rugby, cricket and athletics, notwithstanding that they hardly ever trained together, if at all. To a Corinthian, training was almost considered cheating. G. O. Smith was their brilliant centre-forward and captain of England. He later recollected: 'The Corinthians of my day never trained, and I can say that the need of it was never felt. We were all fit, and I think could have played on for more than one and a half hours without being any the worst.'

The Corinthians often only met up on the day of a match and yet would regularly thrash even the best professional sides. The Dewar Shield was an annual match between the best amateur and the best professional teams of the year. To give you some idea of how good the Corinthians were, in the early 1880s Blackburn won the FA Cup three times running, and in each of those years the Corinthians played Blackburn and beat them. In 1904 they beat Bury 10–3 when Bury were the FA Cup holders!

The following is an extract from a 1906 magazine article on the Corinthians. Modern players and managers, please note: 'The Corinthian style has, I think, always been unique, and never entirely absent, even in the club's worst years. The chief thing about it is the "straight ahead" theory. The forwards play a good open game, without any crowding, taking the ball on the run and making straight for goal without dallying. The passing is crisp, quick, and along the ground; the shooting is done from all angles. There is plenty of hard charging, but never a suspicion of foul play. There is any amount of life and go, and no one ever slacks. In fact, the impression one gleans from watching the Corinthians is that they play to win the game and to enjoy themselves while doing it.'

The last sentence encapsulates the 'Corinthian spirit'. The Corinthians were 'gentlemen', at a time when being a gentleman really meant something. To the Corinthians and many other amateur players, the new penalty law implied a slur upon their moral behaviour on the field, and they raised a spirited opposition to it which lasted for some years. N. L. Jackson, who had founded the Corinthians in 1883, strongly opposed the penalty's introduction in 1891. He thought it was an insult to the honour of a gentleman to suggest he would either deliberately commit a foul or stoop to take advantage of an opponent's transgression. C. B. Fry, perhaps the most illustrious Corinthian of them all, believed it: 'A standing insult to sportsmen to have to play under a rule which assumes that players intend to trip, hack and push opponents and to behave like cads of the most unscrupulous kidney.'

It should be pointed out that not everyone thought the Corinthians were as sporting and as noble as history now portrays them. In his 1898 book entitled *Association Football*, John Goodall recalls a match when the Corinthians were on tour, playing a big holiday fixture: '. . . the brothers Walter at back were thoroughly holding in check the opposite wing men, and their task was rendered no less easy by reason of the encroachment of the spectators, who considerably reduced the field of play. Once, A. M. heavily charged his man into the people, whereupon an old lady, bristling with rage, and ominously presenting an umbrella, advanced upon the Corinthian and threatened to administer chastisement for an attack upon her son! These were the old days. Even old ladies better understand the game now.'

Some critics found the 'holier than thou' attitude something of a pose. On one of their northern tours, a Lancashire paper noted that the Corinthians systematically indulged in rough play and 'were the most dangerous and cruel team that ever opposed provincial footballers'. (Obviously a Blackburn supporter!)

Whatever the truth, the fact remained that as late as 1902 penalty kicks were still not recognized by Corinthians and other amateur players. Penalties were considered a section of the penal code applicable only to the professional game. Gentlemen did not commit fouls!

Put in modern parlance, the Corinthians 'didn't do penalties'. If they were awarded a penalty they would not attempt to score from it. If they had a penalty awarded against them (a rare occurrence) their keeper would not attempt to save it. He would simply stand to one side and allow the kicker to shoot into an open goal!

I must confess, when I first read about this attitude towards penalties (and, in some instances, free-kicks too), I didn't really believe it. But, to my surprise, research proved it was true. It seems that Corinthian penalty takers may well have gently passed the ball to the goalkeeper rather than attempt to score, and that Corinthian keepers stood nonchalantly by a corner flag or post, smoking cigarettes while the kicker stroked the ball into the empty net! It brought to mind the brilliant sketch by Harry Enfield, involving a match between the modern

Liverpool team and an Arsenal team of the early 1900s. As Liverpool, led by John Barnes, warmed up, the Arsenal players smoked pipes and drank beer. At the start of the game Enfield, the Arsenal skipper, tried to hand round sandwiches and cakes to the Liverpool players, who ignored him, swept upfield and scored.

Penalty kick: not intended for 'gentlemen' players!

Deliberate Misses

Even modern-day, hard-nosed professionals have deliberately missed penalties. Robbie Fowler of Liverpool, of course, did his 'Corinthian' impersonation, refusing (unsuccessfully) a penalty awarded to him for an alleged trip by David Seaman of Arsenal, and then hitting a pretty pathetic penalty which Seaman saved, only for Jason McAteer to score from the rebound. But what about this confession from George Hardwick, one of the finest players ever to wear an England shirt, recounted in *Kicking and Screaming*: 'I don't think there could ever have been a team [England 1946–48] in the history of football that entertained so much, because that's what we set out to do: "Now, all these people have paid all this money, let's show them, let's give 'em a show, let's do it." If we scored one, I'm screaming at them, "Now two, two, two, come on let's go, let's go." When we got two I was screaming for three, and I was screaming for four, then five, and the only time I got a little bit upset with myself was when we were beating Holland 8–0 and we got a penalty and I hadn't the guts to score with it. I just knocked it at the goalkeeper. I thought, "Oh no, no, no, we've got eight." I hadn't the heart to go for nine.'

Examples from the modern game are, admittedly, a little more difficult to find, but there is one, involving one of the world's greatest players – Roberto Baggio.

Baggio started his Serie A career with Fiorentina, and Fiorentina stuck by him when he twice broke down with cruciate ligament trouble. So he had a soft spot for the club, and their fans adored him. Sadly, however, a financial crisis forced the Florence side to sell Baggio to Juventus, for a then world-record fee of $11 million. The Florentine fans demonstrated for two days after the transfer, and Baggio himself appeared sad at the move. But no one knew quite how sad he was until six months later.

Juventus met Fiorentina in a league match, Juventus were awarded a penalty and Baggio was by then the regular Juve penalty taker. He refused to take it! The Juve coach was furious and immediately substituted him. Baggio left the pitch wearing a Fiorentina scarf to rapturous applause. It's amazing how cool you can be when you are the best (and most expensive) footballer in the world.

Catch It Hot!

Considerable exception may have been taken to the penalty's introduction by this so-called 'better class' of players, who felt it an insult to their dignity to have to play under such a rule, but as the good book *Association Football and the Men Who Made It* puts it: 'A larger number of sensible fellows who knew that to err was human, and that angels' wings did not grow on the football field, took the new regulation at its face value, and held it to be a blot on the escutcheons of their clubs to have a penalty kick awarded against them. After the penalty's introduction, there is a record of at least one Army officer who took a very dim view of any soldier in his team who was responsible for a penalty being awarded against his regiment. The officer, who was also the playing captain of the regiment's football team, notified in the regulations at the barracks on match days that if the team had a penalty kick given against it, this would be considered a "disgrace to the regiment". Moreover, the offender would, "Catch it hot!"'

Fine sentiment, but sadly, it did not prevail. The author continues: 'Had the rule been taken and acted on everywhere in this spirit it might have had a more salutary effect, but the manner in which many of the paid experts viewed it soon robbed it of its sting. Their policy was to win if possible by fair methods; but when it came to losing, rules were looked at as things to be broken, and the referee to be defied just so far as it was safe to do this. It is not just perhaps for the average reader to cast stones at the professional. There was a good deal of human nature in his actions, and he was egged on by an unthinking and partisan and exceedingly "patriotic" crowd of supporters, who by adjudging the lucky saving of a penalty kick to be a matter for applause, gave it unstintingly, and this confirmed the offenders in their astute private ideas that the means justified the end in football. Had the public taken a just and honest line, and cried down ill deeds, the players would dare not commit them.'

He could almost have been reporting any modern-day professional match, but this was written in 1906, about the introduction of the penalty kick some fifteen years earlier. The Corinthians may have decried the new penalty law as morally bankrupt, and army officers considered it worthy of court martial but, human nature being what it is, just about everyone else tried to get round it. As with most new laws, what was fine in principle and in theory was something quite different in reality. The new law quickly ran into difficulties.

One final illustration, although absolutely nothing to do with penalties, as to how good a side the Corinthians were:

It was December 1894, and the Corinthians were playing at Leyton as part of their annual Christmas tour. After 15 minutes, a thick fog enveloped the ground but the game continued for a short time because the Corinthians were 'penning their opponents in their goal'. At last the referee stopped the game and the players and spectators retired. The two teams were virtually dressed and leaving for the post-match celebration when it was discovered that the Corinthians' goalkeeper was missing. An expedition was sent back out on to the pitch and discovered the keeper still standing between his posts, thinking what a good time his forwards must be having, and wondering how many goals they had scored!

2 – An American in Belfast

Trivia alert: the first ever goal from a penalty kick was scored by J. Dalton, an American born in Ireland, who was playing for the Canadians against Linfield FC in Belfast, in August 1891.

'We are satisfied the public do not grumble at the early commencement of the football season. Perhaps they rather enjoy an autumn's day lounging at a good match to prowling about the city jingling those shillings that cannot be expended, as there is nothing to lay them out upon.'

Thus began the *Belfast Telegraph* match report of the Canadians v Linfield match played on 29 August 1891. The report is a classic – whatever the reporter was on when he wrote it, I wish I could get some: 'A football match in the summer is a godsend to grand-stand players, for they can loll at ease, smoke the pipe of peace – for peace it is at the present – only at the present . . .'

Before going on to describe the players and the match itself, the reporter noted that: 'For the second time in the history of Irish Association football the ladies, or their cavaliers, were requested to pay. This course was adopted in view of the alleged fact that the girls had taken such an interest in the boys on the "arena", such an absorbing interest in foul play, or the new rule for goal-mouth handballs, that they would attend today, and combine pleasure at their favourites winning with gratification at the "fetch" accomplished by late summer costumes . . .'

He then went on to give brief descriptions of the Americans on the Canadian team, noting that 'the Yankees wore a silk scarf', and then saying this about Dalton: 'A quick player is J. Dalton, the centre-half, who is 5ft 9in, with the tidy weight of 175lbs. It is a remarkable fact that his nationality is Irish in the first instance . . .'

The match report itself is, like many other match reports of this time, incredibly detailed. Either these reporters had amazing memories, or they were brilliant at shorthand. The penalty incident is described as follows: 'Gordon the younger gave a handball in goal-mouth, unintentionally it appeared to us. The new rule was immediately put into force, and the players having got twelve yards before the post, Dalton, of the Americans, kicked the ball through, and scored the second goal easily. It can be understood when it did not require the leather to be touched, and there was only one man to stop him . . . The match, taken as a whole, was a very good one, and was exciting from start to finish . . . There was one example of the working of the new foul-in-goal, but we think the referee erred in this case, and that only a free-kick should have been awarded. By his decision Linfield lost a goal. The rule says, if we mistake not, "deliberate". In the case today there were merely an accidental handball, as the leather was kicked against the Linfield player. We have not heard anyone yet say that the rule was rightly put into force. New laws are worth reading, and worth studying also.'

The *Belfast Newsletter* reporter was also of the view that the penalty decision was a harsh one: 'Shortly after this a handball in the goal-mouth was given by Gordon, apparently quite unintentionally, and the players having got twelve yards before the posts, under the new rule Dalton, for Canada, kicked the ball through, and amidst great applause secured the second goal for the visitors.'

It is ironic that the first ever penalty may have been wrongly awarded.

The first successful penalty in senior English football was scored for Newton Heath (Lancashire and Yorkshire Railway) against Blackpool in a Lancashire League game on 5 September 1891 (Newton Heath, of course, later became the best-known football club in the world – Manchester United): '. . . And from a free-kick Newton Heath put the ball through the posts, but it did not touch anyone in transit. Cookson now made a grand attempt, his shot hitting the upright, but the ball was cleared. Newton relieved, and from a rush Donaldson was pulled off the ball by Woods in front of goal, and the referee (Mr T. Hulme, of Farnworth) allowed a penalty kick, this being taken by Farman, who had no difficulty in beating Wright . . . The home team was lucky to make a draw, as their goal was got from a penalty kick . . . Several of the Heathen supporters were betting on Blackpool, and all admitted that they had hard lines in not winning. The penalty kick did the trick.'

The first man to score with a penalty kick in the Football League is generally held to have been James Heath, for Wolves against Accrington, on 14 September 1891. The *Wolverhampton Express and Star* reported: 'A scrimmage in the Reds' quarters led to a thoroughly interesting point of the game, a point which local spectators had never previously seen put in force in a League match, the putting into operation of the new rule of the Association which forbids deliberate foul play twelve yards from goal. The kick was taken, everyone of the other players standing six yards behind the twelve-yard line, except the opposing goalkeeper, and a very easy point was scored, McVickers having not the remotest chance of stopping the shot.'

The *Birmingham Daily Gazette* gave a few more details: 'A hot attack followed on the Accrington goal, and after the ball had been shot in twice at close quarters, Heath put it over the line. A foul, however, had been claimed for the second shot, which was by Devey. One of the Accrington half-backs had acted as goalkeeper for the occasion, and the new rule which gives a free-kick to the attacking side with no one but the defending goalkeeper in front was enforced. Heath took the kick and sent the ball clean through with a low hard shot, Hay failing to hold it altogether. This according to the new rule thus made the second goal for the Wanderers.'

Trivia alert: the hitherto accepted wisdom that Heath's penalty for Wolves was the first to be scored in the Football League may not in fact be true. At the bottom of the same page as the Wolves report, in a brief report on a match between Leicester Fosse and Notts County, is the following reference: 'Morel scored twice and Bailey once for Fosse, the latter scoring from a free-kick under the new rule . . .'

So, you heard it here first: Heath may not have been the first League penalty scorer – Mr Bailey of Leicester may have beaten him to it. Do I know how to party or what?! I hope to have discovered the exact starting times of these two matches by the time the paperback version of the book comes out, and thus resolve this burning issue once and for all. Stay tuned.

All these penalties had one thing in common, which made them collectors' items in the 1890s – they actually resulted in a goal. Successfully converted penalties quickly became a rarity.

Too Many Saves

Part of the reason for there being too many saves was possibly the short list of offences for which a penalty could be awarded. New offences were added to the list on a fairly regular basis, but there was always something which wasn't covered or situations where the law was ambiguous. The main difficulty, however, was players didn't worry unduly about committing any of the fouls devised by the International Board. For a long time after its introduction, outfield players (and goalkeepers) were quite relaxed about conceding a penalty for one simple reason – goalkeepers saved most of them.

That the penalty was plagued by keepers making too many saves may seem a little odd to us today. In the 1994 World Cup in the United States of America, fifteen (non-shoot-out) penalties were awarded in normal time and not one was missed or saved.

There is no such statistical evidence from the late-Victorian era, but there is sufficient anecdotal material to conclude with certainty that the odds then were much more in favour of the goalkeeper. For many years the new law was a failure when viewed in terms of the mischief it was intended to prevent. Strange, therefore, that the authorities took almost fourteen years before seriously attempting to make life more difficult for goalkeepers and more in favour of penalty takers.

The Early Years

The initial stage of the penalty kick's life consisted mostly of tinkering with side-issues, and consideration of well-meant but slightly weird suggestions from the clubs and other Home Associations, rather than dealing with the fundamental problems. The first change to the penalty law, in 1892, is a perfect example. With all the loopholes perforating the first draft the International Board came up with this: 'deliberately' handling the ball was changed to 'wilfully' handling the ball.

'Big deal,' you might well say, but this amendment is a further reminder of the original impetus behind the law – the desire more to punish ungentlemanly play as opposed to limiting what we would consider rough or dangerous play.

A player could 'deliberately' handle the ball and still not intend to cheat – protecting your face from being struck by the ball, for example. The authorities wanted to crack down on cheating, and 'wilfully' seemed more appropriate to the circumstances. The dictionary definition of 'wilful' contains references to 'malice', 'evil intent' and other words suggesting that if you are wilful you are a bounder and a rotter.

The authorities didn't appreciate that deciding whether a particular handball was wilful, as opposed to merely deliberate, required a judgement inappropriate to a football field. Yet again, the poor referee had to implement an ambiguous law in the face of hostile players and crowds and, yet again, many ducked the issue in the interests of self-preservation. It was not until 1899–1900 that the wording was changed to 'intentionally'. (The wording was actually changed back to 'deliberate' later, and this is still the current law, although the guidance notes for referees still require the referee to assess the intention behind any handling of the ball.)

It is a mystery how 'pushing' an opponent could have been omitted from the first draft of the law but it certainly was. For the real villains of Victorian football this was a bit of a lifeline. Just as the striker is about to shoot for goal, you casually wander over, shove him on to the ground, and all the referee can do is award a free-kick. To be fair, this was quickly remedied and, in 1893, the relevant section was changed to read 'trip, or hold, or push'. Of course, it remained perfectly in order to kick, strike, charge or jump at an opponent, but it was a start.

Another important change to occur in this post-natal period was the addition of a clause authorizing the extension of playing time to allow a penalty kick to be taken. This amendment was a direct result of another defeat suffered by Stoke City in a Cup match, this time at the hands of Aston Villa.

On 21 November 1891, Stoke were losing 2–1 when they were awarded a penalty with a minute or so to go before full-time. The Villa keeper had the ball and, showing great enterprise, or cynicism if you are a Stoke supporter, hoofed it as far as he could out of the ground. It seems the individuals sent to retrieve the ball quickly cottoned on to what was happening and took their own sweet time in returning it. As a result the ninety minutes expired before the kick could be taken. There being no provision in the law for the game to be extended for a penalty, and the referee (wisely, given Villa were at home) showing no inclination to make one up on the spot, the game was over and Stoke lost. The law was changed the following year, and the referee was authorized to extend time to allow a penalty to be taken, both at half-time and at the end of ninety minutes.

The early period of the penalty law was also notable for the changes which were proposed but rejected. Having met with such initial opposition, suddenly everyone now had ideas on how to make the penalty kick more effective. Burnley FC proposed that the penalty kick be taken 'from the 12-yard mark at a point directly opposite to that where the infringement took place'. So, get fouled near the corner flag and you would be taking your penalty from near the touchline. The International Board minutes dryly note that the suggestion 'was not entertained'.

The Scottish FA tried on more than one occasion to have the penalty area extended to 30 yards from the goal-line. It makes you wonder what on earth was going on in the Scottish game at that time to warrant such an authoritarian approach – relative order within the penalty areas and complete mayhem everywhere else! The Scots also tried, equally unsuccessfully, to reinstate the referee's discretion to award a penalty only if he thought a goal would have resulted but for the foul.

More sensibly, in April 1894, Aston Villa put forward a proposal limiting the penalty area to a space 12 yards from the goal-line and 12 yards from each side of the goalposts. The penalty box was born, albeit a baby-sized version.

The Pitch

Immediately prior to the introduction of the penalty kick, the layout of a football pitch was pretty basic. Mind you, it could have been designed by Leonardo da Vinci when compared to the 'pitches' used in those marvellous medieval contests, some of which are still re-enacted today, where the goals are miles apart and the game itself is more akin to war than sport.

A quick historical diversion, courtesy of Desmond Morris' *The Soccer Tribe* and Young's *History of British Football.* In those medieval games, the 'goal' was the object to which the ball had to be carried to win the game, and the nature of this object varied from place to place. In the All Saints' versus St Peter's match in Derby, the All Saints' goal was the water-wheel of Nun's Mill, which had to be knocked three times for a goal. The St Peter's goal was a nursery gate about a mile out of town. When the ball was touched on to one of these 'goals' it was said to have been 'goaled'. The victorious player did not score a goal; he 'goaled a goal'. These games (pitch-battles would be more accurate) were, in fact, the original Golden Goal matches. The first goal won the match, although it was quite common for no goal to be scored at all. There was no such thing as 'Ye Olde Penaltye Shoote Oute'.

When posts started to be used, the players had to drive the ball between the posts or carry it past them. This meant it was easier to score, and so games were no longer decided by one goal but by the most goals scored within a given period. It therefore became necessary to keep a record as the game proceeded and, initially, this was done by cutting notches in the wood of the goalposts. The cutting or 'scoring' of the goalposts led to the introduction of the phrase 'scoring a goal'. At first this referred to the recording of the score, but gradually changed to mean the act of scoring itself. So, all of football's current problems with drawn matches are in fact the fault of whoever came up with the idea of goalposts.

Without them, every football match would still be 'sudden death'.

By 1863, the date of the first officially sanctioned pitch, things had progressed from mill wheels and carving notches in goalposts, but the pitch still only bore a passing resemblance to the modern pitch. Rule 1 (dimensions of the playing area) stated the maximum length and breadth of the pitch – 200 yards and 100 yards respectively – and little else.

These old pitches look very much like those my brother and I used to play on in the playing field behind my house when I was a boy in Stafford. Not the two sweaters we used for the posts, but the almost complete lack of visible boundaries. Remember those games of two-a-side or 'three and in'? Two players almost disappearing from view, engaged in their own private dribbling battle, while the rest of us sat down and waited for them to return. Well, it was similar in the 1860s: only the corners of the pitch were required to be marked out (by flags), although some free-thinking clubs also added flags along the sides of the pitches. The freedom of wingers to roam far and wide was often only curtailed by the ever-increasing number of spectators gathered at the side of the pitch. In an early game played in Nottingham, there is a story of one player who scored by breaking through the hedge and running through the adjacent field.

Proper touchlines – so called because in the earliest days of the game when the ball went over the line it was the first player (of either side) who touched it who was allowed to bring it back into play – were only introduced in 1883, the same year in which the use of tape for the crossbar was no longer officially recognized.

Following the introduction of the penalty kick, the law regarding the layout of the pitch was formally changed and 'lines defining 6 yards from the goalposts, and 12 and 18 yards from the goal-line' were now required to be marked out. The new 'penalty' pitch looked as follows:

Football at the Crystal Palace. The Cup Final of 1901.
An anxious moment after a corner kick

I suspect some readers are looking at this photograph and thinking, 'The groundsman must have been some sort of pervert: why else is there a pair of breasts where the six-yard box should be?' Yet that was the six-yard box. Drawing lines 'six yards from the goalposts' does not produce a neat rectangle – it produces the shape you see in the photograph above. My sympathies go out to the groundsmen in the 1890s – it must have been a real pain marking-out a breast-shaped six-yard area.

The rest of the layout is easy to follow. As we know, the penalty area stretched right across the pitch, 12 yards from the goal-line, and the dotted line marked a spot 18 yards from the goal-line, so the referee could make sure all the other players were six yards behind the kicker. It was not actually mandatory to mark out the 18-yard line until the 1901–02 season, although most senior clubs did so. The centre-circle and centre spot were also introduced for the first time in 1892.

Spurs v. Sheffield United. The Cup Final of 1901 – 114,000 watch Willie Foulke retrieve the ball from the back of Sheffield United's net

The pitch layout remained like this until 1902, a key moment in football history, when the entire Laws of the Game, and particularly the laws relating to the pitch and the penalty kick, underwent some fundamental changes. However, prior to 1902 some important amendments were also made to the substantive part of the penalty law, which, for the sake of good order, are summarized below:

- In 1896–97 'charge from behind' was added to the list of fouls; 'on appeal' was deleted and the word 'shall' substituted, i.e., the referee had to award a penalty if any relevant offence was committed. The ball also had to be kicked forward to be in play.
- In 1899–1900 the rule regarding handball was changed from 'wilfully' to 'intentionally'.
- In 1901–02 'kick' and 'jump at' were added to the list of fouls.

- In the same season the International Board minuted the following: 'If a goalkeeper has been changed without the referee being notified, and the new goalkeeper handles the ball within the 12-yards line, a penalty kick must be awarded . . . in the event of the ball touching the goalkeeper before passing between the posts when a penalty kick is being taken at the expiry of time, a goal is scored.'
- The 1902 rule book also noted the following recommendation and decision of the International Board: 'Recommendation – Cases of handling the ball and tripping, pushing, kicking or holding an opponent and charging an opponent from behind, may so happen as to be considered unintentional, and when this is so, no penalty must be awarded. Decision – A penalty kick can be awarded irrespective of the position of the ball at the time the offence is committed.

Of greater interest, England were awarded their first international penalty, against Ireland, in 1899. Jimmy Crabtree took it and missed. The miss had little bearing on the result (England won 13–2) but if Crabtree had scored, England would have scored more goals than in any one game before or since. It was also a personal disaster for Crabtree – he never scored for England.

Wailing Banshees

The 1902–03 changes started with Law 1 – the law dealing with the field of play. The modern pitch was born: 'Lines shall be marked 6 yards from each goalpost at right angles to the goal-lines for a distance of 6 yards, and these shall be connected with each other by a line parallel to the goal-line; the space within these lines shall be the goal-area. Lines shall be marked 18 yards from each goalpost at right angles to the goal-lines for a distance of 18 yards, and these shall be connected with each other by a line parallel to the goal-lines; the space within these lines shall be the penalty area. A suitable mark shall be made opposite the centre of each goal, 12 yards from the goal-line; this shall be the penalty-kick mark.'

So, an 18-yard box, a rectangular six-yard area, a penalty spot and not a breast in sight! The only thing missing was the arc at the top of the penalty area, and for that we need a brief jump forward to 1923.

Until I started researching this book I had no idea why there was an arc at the top of the penalty area. For nearly thirty-odd years I simply accepted its presence without a moment's thought. Actually, it was introduced to prevent the defending players all lining up directly behind the penalty taker and restricting his run-up to six yards. The change to the law in 1923 required all players, with the exception of the player taking the penalty kick and the opponents' goalkeeper, to be outside the penalty area, 'and at least 10 yards from where the kick is being taken'.

Back to 1902. Law 16 was now the penalty-kick law, and it read as follows: 'In the event of any intentional infringement of Law 10 by the defending side within the penalty area, the referee shall award the opponents a penalty kick which shall be taken from the penalty-kick mark under the following conditions: All players, with the exception of the player taking the kick and the opponents' goalkeeper, shall be outside the penalty area. *The opponents' goalkeeper shall be within the goal area.* The ball must be kicked forward. The ball shall be in play when the kick is taken, and a goal may be scored from a penalty kick; but the ball shall not be played again by the kicker until it has been played by another player. If necessary, time shall be extended to admit of a penalty kick being taken.'

The italics are mine, and highlight a missed opportunity. Once again the authorities side-stepped the issue of penalties being too easy to save. All that was required of keepers was that they had to be in the six-yard area – an interesting choice of words. I mean, where else were they going to be? This may have been an indirect reference to our old friends the Corinthians.

Corinthians apart, in reality this was no change at all, given the previous law merely prohibited keepers from advancing beyond the six-yard area. Keepers could, therefore, either charge out of their goal, or stand at the edge of the six-yard box and jump around as much as they liked before the kick was taken. Many did exactly this, leaping about and 'wailing like banshees'. One Rab McFarlane of (Middlesbrough) would wait for the kicker to begin his run-up and then tear off his cap, whirling it around his head while he danced along the goal-line howling complete gibberish in an attempt to put the kicker off. One textbook's advice to keepers in 1898 stated: 'In dealing with a penalty kick – they will happen amongst the best-regulated teams – it is better to come out the full six yards. Some of the best goalkeepers make a practice of dancing about extravagantly and waving their arms to disconcert the kicker. Be prepared if the ball is gently tipped over your head – it is an easy kick.'

The last sentence refers to the unique penalty-taking technique developed by several players to combat the problem of keepers rushing out to the edge of the six-yard area. They became adept at lifting the ball over the keeper's head and into the goal. Remember Karel Poborsky's great goal for the Czech Republic against Portugal in Euro '96? Poborsky would have been a natural penalty taker in the early 1900s.

Law 10 was now the law which contained the offences for which a referee *had* to award a penalty kick. It read as follows: 'Neither tripping, kicking nor jumping at a player shall be allowed. A player, the goalkeeper excepted, shall not intentionally handle the ball under any pretence whatever. A player shall not use his hands to hold or push an opponent. A player shall not be charged from behind, unless he is facing his own goal, and is also intentionally impeding an opponent.'

The eagle-eyed among you may have spotted what appears to be a fundamental error in the above section. In their laudable enthusiasm to clarify the handball rule, the authorities drafted a law which, on a literal reading, allowed goalkeepers to handle the ball anywhere on the pitch. Surely, this could not be right.

Indeed it was. It may come as a surprise, but prior to this change keepers could legally handle the ball in their own half of the pitch. However, the new law inadvertently authorized the handling of the ball anywhere on the pitch. Nor was this just a theoretical problem; goalkeepers took advantage of this loophole for many years, culminating in a game between Motherwell and Third Lanark in Scotland in 1910, when both keepers utilized their ability to handle the ball to score a goal. The law was changed in 1913: 'A player (the goalkeeper within his own penalty area excepted), shall not intentionally handle the ball.'

Of slightly more concern was the provision outlawing charging from behind unless the player was facing his own goal. Under this rule it was perfectly lawful to charge someone from behind if he was facing your goal or facing sideways. This was not what the authorities had intended – attackers being charged over from behind because they happened to be facing towards the goal they were attacking. The law was changed in 1904–05 to read: 'A player shall not be charged from behind unless he is intentionally impeding an opponent.'

Advantage

Not a great deal happened between 1903 and 1906 save for one important change to the law in 1903–04, and for the first time 'advantage' became part of football's vocabulary: 'The referee may refrain from putting the provisions of this law into effect where he is satisfied that by enforcing them he would be giving an advantage to the offending side.'

If you are somewhat bemused by the application of an advantage law to the penalty kick, I completely understand. However, the 'provisions' of the law being referred to did indeed include the penalty kick. The crazy truth was the authorities really did want to give the referee the option to play advantage, because awarding a penalty was often perceived to be giving the *offending* side an advantage! As one commentator noted at the time, this new law was: 'A blow at the astute and unprincipled player, who had managed to twist even a law specially imposed to deter him from unfair play to his advantage, for rather than run the risk of losing a goal he preferred to take the chance of a penalty kick, which experience had shown him failed in a large percentage of cases. It was felt that if the player knew that the unfair act would not be certain to give the desired option he would give up committing it.'

Even an advantage law didn't work. In 1904 David Lindsay scored a hat-trick of penalties, and one other goal, all in the second half, to bring St Mirren back from 2–1 down against Rangers and on to win 5–4. The hat-trick of goals from the penalty spot was remarkable in itself, but there was also one other penalty in the match (this was not uncommon – three or four penalties in a match was not unusual). In 1905–06, the International Board allowed goals to be scored direct from free-kicks awarded for certain offences, and finally made a real attempt to sort out those irritating 'Guardians of the Goalposts'. The goalkeeper in late-Victorian football was a player who, in the words of the great Stoke and Welsh international, L. Richmond Roose: 'Should stand six feet and no nonsense!'

Goalkeepers

The popular adage about keepers used to be, 'You don't have to be mad to be a keeper, but it helps.' In the late 1890s and early 1900s it would have read, 'You don't have to be big and mad to be a keeper but it helps.'

Keepers in Victorian football needed to be able to take a lot of punishment. Charging the keeper was not only lawful in those days, it was almost a sport in itself. In the late 1880s it was a recognized form of attack, and was permissible as long as the chargers were onside when the ball was last kicked. That's right, the keeper did not even have to have the ball! A report of an early Corinthian match describes a goal scored 'from a fine middle by Bambridge . . . Dewhurst having previously disposed of the goalkeeper.'

Preston North End were, apparently, masters of this tactic: 'A half-back, carefully judging the time to pass, would kick the ball in the air in the direction of the goalkeeper, who would at once be attacked by two of the inside-forwards, while the third would attempt to slip past the backs and shoot into the empty goal.'

The references to 'disposing' of the goalkeeper, or 'attacking him', are not simply poetic licence on the part of the reporter. Several cases of serious injury and, believe it or not, two of death, had occurred owing to the custom of one or more players 'laying the goalkeeper out', so as to prepare the way for a more successful attack on goal.

Some relief was provided in 1893, when the laws were changed so a keeper could only be charged when he was in the act of playing the ball or obstructing an opponent. One commentator of the time noted that this change 'freed the keeper from the attention of the goal-rusher, whose duties were almost entirely confined to disposing of the goalkeeper whenever the ball came within 20 yards of the goal'.

This was not entirely true. The keeper could still be charged if he was playing the ball or holding it. As you can imagine, there were few problems with goalkeepers hanging on to the ball and slowing up play in Victorian times. In the 1887 FA Cup Final between Aston Villa and West Bromwich, it was noted that only the brave goalkeeping of the Villa keeper Warner kept out the West Bromwich forwards, and that, 'On more than one occasion he scooped the ball up and over his own crossbar to avoid being bundled into the goal.'

So, to play in goal you either had to be a psychopath or a complete masochist. Most keepers appear to have been large psychopaths with masochistic tendencies. And the biggest of them all was the great, the legendary, Willie Foulke.

'Little Willie'

Willie Foulke was probably the largest man ever to play professional football. He played for England, Sheffield United, Chelsea and Bradford City, and would make Peter Schmeichel look like a schoolboy! If ever Professor Hawkins perfects time travel I'm going back to see Willie play, and then I'm going to kidnap him and ask him to play for Spurs in the Premiership. I suspect kidnapping Willie Foulke would require a whole company of the SAS, though. When he began his career he weighed 15 stone. He ended it at 22 stone 3 pounds (311 pounds). He was 6 feet 3 inches tall, wore size 12 boots, 24-inch collars and his nickname was 'Little Willie' or 'Fatty Foulke', although not many people called him either to his face. In the first ever Chelsea programme in 1905 he is described as follows: '"Little Willie" aged 29 and a half stands 6 feet 3 inches, weighs 22 stone and is as fine a specimen of manhood as ever stepped on the field . . . In spite of his bulk he possesses all the activity of a cat, combined with all the playfulness of a kitten.'

Legend has it this 'kitten' could carry a man under each arm and could punch a football – the old heavy leather ones – to the halfway line (heaven only knows how far he would punch a modern ball). In 1899, while playing for Sheffield United in the FA Cup, Little Willie made a brilliant, game-saving stop, only to tear a thigh muscle in the process. It took six men to carry him from the field – the stretchers weren't big enough.

At Chelsea, where he only played one season (in 1905–06), but was a cult hero nevertheless, he weighed almost as much as his two full-backs combined. If you don't believe me take a look at this picture.

Little Willie taking up the whole goalmouth at Stamford Bridge. Note the ballboy by Willie's left-hand post

Foulke was the first ever Chelsea goalkeeper because he joined the first ever Chelsea team. The football team was actually an afterthought to the Stamford Bridge stadium itself, which had been built by the Mears brothers to stage big matches such as the FA Cup Final, which was played at Stamford Bridge three times in the early 1920s. The team was put together in a few months, comprising mainly Scottish imports and the great Foulke, who joined from Sheffield United.

Look again at the Chelsea team photo. In the background, behind the right-hand goalpost, you can just make out the small figure of a ball-boy. The story goes that, to intimidate the opposition by drawing attention to Foulke's huge size,

Little Willie in all his 22-stone glory

Chelsea had him take the field with two small boys who would stand behind his goal. Once these boys started retrieving the ball the 'ball-boy' was invented.

Little Willie appears to have enjoyed his stay in London – he was over 26 stone when he left, and was often seen in the trendy clothes shops along the Fulham and King's roads. He fancied himself as a bit of a dandy, and in the winter used to wear a silk scarf with a gold pin proclaiming himself 'King Custodian'.

It came as no surprise to discover that Little Willie's eating habits were as legendary as his goalkeeping. There is one story concerning a Chelsea away match, involving the team in an overnight stay in a hotel. When the rest of the team came down for dinner, they found eleven empty plates – Foulke, having got the time for dinner wrong, had consoled himself at the lack of dinner companions by eating all the food before the others arrived.

Despite his size, Foulke was an agile and talented keeper and, apparently, a great captain. He was worth the admission money on his own, irrespective of what happened in the match, and always drew a big crowd. On one occasion, when he felt his defence had really let him down, he refused to make any more saves. Nor did he like opposing strikers very much; they tended to irritate him, which was not a good idea. On one occasion, he picked up an opposing forward and threw him into the net, deliberately conceding a penalty. Another time, during the 1898–99 season, he picked up Liverpool centre-forward George Allan, turned him upside down and stood him on his head in the mud, again seemingly quite content to give away the spot kick.

Willie was the complete opposite to those amateur players who thought the penalty law immoral. While Corinthian goalkeepers stood quietly to one side, Willie and his chums charged out of the goal to the edge of the six-yard area, yelling and screaming and making it almost impossible to score. On his debut for Chelsea he saved a penalty against

Stockport, only for the rebound to be put away by a player following up. One Burton Albion opponent is alleged to have complained, after missing his second penalty of a match against Chelsea, that there was no room either side of Foulke at which to shoot.

Ironically, and rather sadly, Foulke spent his final years in Blackpool, scratching a living by inviting members of the public to score against him in a 'Beat Little Willie' penalty challenge. He died in Blackpool in May 1916, from pneumonia contracted while saving penalties for pennies. He was only 40 years old.

Still Too Many Saves

With his extraordinary physical presence, Little Willie may have been the extreme example, but the problem was commonplace: keepers were saving far too many penalty kicks. As a result, players continued to foul in order to prevent a goal being scored, confident that in many cases the resulting penalty kick would not yield a goal. So in 1905, Law 16 was changed in an attempt to make the keeper's life a little more difficult: 'The opponents' goalkeeper shall not advance beyond his own goal-line.'

OK, so it wasn't much, but it was on the right lines – it just didn't go far enough. Keepers could no longer charge out at the penalty taker, or stand on the edge of the six-yard box, but they could still move before the ball was kicked, and many still charged out a bit – old habits die hard. While the more law-abiding keepers used the right to move to get a little way off their line, or to dance around in order to confuse the kicker, in practice many still managed to get forward enough to block the shot. In 1912, in a Second Division match between Chelsea and Glossop, the Glossop keeper, Butler, saved a penalty but was adjudged by the referee to have moved forward before the ball was kicked, and the penalty was ordered to be retaken. Butler was so incensed at this decision he argued too much with the referee and was sent off.

A further problem had arisen in relation to infringements committed by the defending side while a penalty was being taken, such as encroachment into the penalty area before the ball was kicked. Some referees could not decide what to do if a defender committed a foul while the penalty was being taken but a goal was scored nevertheless. Should the goal stand or should the penalty to be retaken? This was a real dilemma given the difficulties of actually scoring from a penalty kick. A further amendment dealt with this specific point: 'If when a penalty kick is taken the ball passes between the goalposts, under the bar, the goal shall not be nullified by reason of any infringement by the defending side.'

The law on charging continued to cause problems and Law 9 was amended yet again. This resulted in the first ever reference to dangerous or violent play: 'Charging is permissible, but it must not be violent or dangerous. A player shall not be charged from behind unless he is intentionally obstructing an opponent.'

Between 1906 and 1929 there were very few changes to the law. However, in 1910 the first penalty in an FA Cup Final was awarded and, amazingly, a goal was actually scored from it. The replayed Final between Newcastle and Barnsley at Goodison Park was a classic example of how rough a game of football was in those days. Newcastle were the main offenders: early on in the game, Newcastle's striker, Higgins, flattened the Barnsley keeper Mearns, who had to be restrained by the referee and a team-mate when he tried to chase after Higgins to exact his revenge. A little later, even the Newcastle team appear to have been unhappy with one of their number after he had kicked Barnsley's right-back, Downs, in the stomach, causing him to be carried off.

It was ironic that the penalty was awarded for a trip on Higgins, the worst offender of the first half. Albert Shepherd, scorer of Newcastle's first goal, duly converted the kick, thus becoming the first player to score a penalty in an FA Cup Final.

In 1914–15 'striking' was added to the list of fouls, but otherwise nothing else of note changed. The core problem, however, remained: goalkeepers were still saving too many penalties. A match between Grimsby and Burnley in February 1909 is the perfect example. Reduced to ten men after only a few minutes due to injury (there were no substitutes in those days), Grimsby went one down after 16 minutes to a goal by Walter Abbott. Then, in a ten-minute period before half-time, Grimsby conceded three penalties in quick succession.

Cause for serious alarm one might have thought, but the Grimsby team were not unduly worried. You see, Walter Scott, their keeper, was something of a penalty-saving expert – he had saved seven out of eight penalties in the preceding two months. He was so good at saving penalties that some commentators believed the Grimsby players were positively reckless about giving them away, so confident were they Scott would make a save.

As expected, Scott saved the first penalty, only for the defence to concede another a few minutes later. Scott saved this one as well, but one of his defenders handled the ball in the resulting goal-mouth scramble. The first two attempts had been taken by Dick Smith, but Abbott took the third, and this time Scott was beaten. He was, apparently, just a wee bit miffed with his defence!

After the interval Grimsby were temporarily reduced to nine men when Whitehouse left the field for 'repairs to his knickers', whereupon they conceded another penalty. This time Scott's job was relatively simple – Abbott's shot came straight at him and he made an easy save. Grimsby still lost, but only 2–0. The match report noted: 'Scott had the distinction of preventing three out of four penalty kicks taking effect – a record for the ground, I think. It appears he had previously earned a good reputation in this line of business. It is no exaggeration to describe Scott's behaviour in goal as the outstanding feature of the game, and the crowd accorded him an ovation at the interval and afterwards in recognition of his masterly display.'

In 1912 Manchester City missed three penalties in the same League match (Eli Fletcher two; Irvine Thornley one) which cost them a win against Newcastle, who drew 2–2. Coincidentally, and far worse, City went into the last match of the 1925–26 season needing a draw at Newcastle to stay in the First Division, and were leading 2–1 when their England winger Billy Austin missed a penalty that would have kept them up. They lost 3–2 and were relegated by a single point. It really wasn't their year. They were the highest-scoring club ever to go down (89 goals) and they lost 1–0 in the FA Cup Final.

Ironically, the greatest number of penalties scored in one season by any individual player is 13, by Francis Lee for Manchester City in the old Division One during the 1971–72 season.

Trivia alert: if anyone asks you how many penalties have been missed in FA Cup Finals, listen very carefully to the way the question is phrased. If they say 'Wembley Cup Finals', you are OK. As everyone knows, the answer is two: Aldridge for Liverpool against Wimbledon in 1988, and Lineker for Spurs against Nottingham Forest in 1991. However, if the question refers simply to Cup Finals, you need to answer 'three'.

The 1913 Cup Final was played at Crystal Palace between Aston Villa and Sunderland, before a then world-record crowd of 120,081. In the first half, Villa's Stephenson was brought down in the box and up stepped Charlie Wallace to take the kick. Ironically, Wallace was the only Sunderland-born player on the pitch, which may or may not have accounted for the fact that he missed the goal by about ten yards. Apparently he was so upset he locked himself in the toilet at half-time.

Wallace need not have been so concerned. He was fated to miss that penalty. His team-mate, Stephenson, already knew Villa were going to win 1–0, but the goal was not going to be a penalty. Stephenson had had a dream about the game and told Sunderland's Buchan the outcome as they waited for a throw-in early on: '1–0. Dreamt it last night. Tommy Barber with a header.'

With a quarter of an hour left, Barber duly made Stephenson's dream come true by heading home a Wallace corner.

Early, Crucial, Cup Final Penalties

The 1922 FA Cup Final at Stamford Bridge between Huddersfield and Preston was a depressing affair, settled by a penalty. There was no doubt that it was a foul – Billy Smith, England's outside-left, was brought down. Equally, there was little doubt that the offence was commited outside the box. However, it was awarded, and Smith got up to score.

The Preston full-back, Hamilton, who had fouled Smith from behind, when Smith was on his way to goal, should have been sent off, and this prompted the commentators to cry 'shame' on Preston, even though the foul was outside the box. The best entertainment of the game was the sight of Huddersfield's bespectaled keeper, J. F. Mitchell, trying to put Smith off by dancing around on the line.

The 1938 Cup Final between the same two sides was the first to go to extra-time, and was the first time a penalty was awarded in a Wembley Cup Final. The game up to the 119th minute had been particularly dull, and fans had already begun to leave when BBC commentator Tom Woodroofe promised his listeners, 'If they score now, I'll eat my hat.' Just at that moment, George Mutch, Preston's Scottish international inside-right, advanced on goal. It looked innocuous enough but England's centre-half, Alf Young, mistimed his tackle and Mutch fell over. There were doubts over whether it was a foul and there were doubts over whether it was in the box, but the ref gave a penalty anyway. Mutch picked himself up and blasted the ball in off the crossbar – producing one of the best penalty photos of all time.

In off the bar. Preston's clincher in the last minute of extra-time in the 1938 Cup Final

In the 1929 Scottish Cup Final, holders Rangers were awarded a penalty in the first half. The previous year, their first goal in a 4–0 win (the first time they'd won the Cup since 1903) had been scored from the penalty spot by Davie Meiklejohn. This time he left the kick to Tom 'Tully' Craig. He shot too close to goalkeeper Sam Clemie and Kilmarnock went on to win the Cup for the last time. If Rangers had won, they'd have taken the Cup three years in a row (1928–30). Craig's miss, as far as records show, was the first in any Scottish Cup Final. And of the first six misses in a Final, five were by Rangers players. Only Craig's affected the game's result, though.

McCrum's Legacy

1929. The year of the Great Wall Street Crash, the beginning of the Great Economic Depression, and the beginning of the end for keepers when it came to saving most penalties: 'The opponents' goalkeeper must stand on his own goal-line until the ball is kicked . . .' read a further amendment to Law 16.

'Stand' is clearly a word goalkeepers had some problem with. The rest of the world interprets 'stand' as meaning to remain in one spot without moving your feet. Goalkeepers, however, believed it meant the complete opposite. They thought it meant jump around, charge forward, jump up and down. This time the authorities were not to be denied. The final blow came the following year: 'The word "stand" means that the goalkeeper must not move his feet until the penalty kick has been taken.'

It had taken nearly forty years but the penalty law had finally become what William McCrum had intended it to be all those years before, in 1891 – an effective punishment for foul play. McCrum lived to see his idea reach fruition but then died, a year later, after a long illness. His legacy is enormous when you think of the world-wide importance of football today, and the importance of the penalty kick within it. He must have been proud to see how central his 'Irishman's motion' became to the overall development of the game, particularly the layout of the playing field. However, not even in his wildest dreams could McCrum have anticipated the birth of 'Son of Penalty Kick' – The Penalty Shoot-Out. Nor could he have contemplated that some sixty-six years after finally getting the penalty kick to work, the authorities would again take pity on goalkeepers and allow them once again to move before the ball is kicked.

To understand why goalkeepers have had their movement restored, and what the penalty shoot-out has to do with a child's party-bag, we need to travel forward to the 1960s, to Zurich, and the home of the game's governing body, FIFA.

3 – Strafschoppen

Tirs au but. Ai rigori anche. Lanzamiento de penalties tambien. Elfmeterschießen. Penalty shoot-outs . . . call them what you will, I love them. The guy(s) who invented the penalty shoot-out (isn't the Dutch word *Strafschoppen* much better?) should have been knighted (after spending years lounging on a beach in the Bahamas, served pina coladas by beautiful models while watching endless reruns of *Cheers*). In fact, I know that before they died they had an even better time – they were paid to travel the world and watch football matches. 'Sad,' as my wife would say, but what does she know?

Why am I such a fan of the penalty shoot-out? And no, it's not simply because it provides another chapter for this book, or because I like watching England lose on penalties. Unlike many Scots, my brother being the perfect example, I support England (unless they are playing Scotland), and I was as disappointed as any English fan when England lost the two most famous shoot-outs ever, in 1990 and 1996.

The Rolling Stones

I have particularly vivid, and rather surreal, memories of the

World Cup semi-final in 1990 between Germany and England. I watched the semi-final, along with 50,000 other people, at Wembley Stadium. The atmosphere was electric, the crowd was tense but well behaved, the— I know, I know – the World Cup was in Italy in 1990. Yet I really did watch the game at Wembley, and there really were 50,000 other people watching with me. I suppose a few of them might have been watching The Rolling Stones, who were playing a concert at the time, but most were watching the England game.

It is a sad reflection on how little chance England were given to succeed in 1990, that The Rolling Stones scheduled one of their Wembley concerts on the same night as a World Cup semi-final. However, courtesy of Platt, Lineker, Gascoigne and Bobby Robson, England made it through to the semi-final against Germany.

I was committed to go to see The Stones with about ten friends. My fiancée was on her 'hen-week' in Rhodes (the details of which are still shrouded in mystery). I managed to see some of the first half in my brother Ken's restaurant in Hampstead then had to go to the concert. We made it on to the Wembley pitch a few minutes into the second-half of the match. It was bizarre. All around me on the hallowed turf (covered in tarpaulins) were guys with mini-televisions or radios, surrounded by other guys (and girls) listening to or watching the match. The Stones were excellent (I think). They had sixty-feet-high, inflatable 'Honky Tonk' women, huge television screens, masses of lasers and lights, and Mick Jagger singing up a storm. And yet a large number of the audience were more interested in football. When Lineker scored the equalizer it nearly stopped the concert.

The penalty shoot-out was unbelievable. By that stage I had given up all pretence of watching the concert. I was trying to get sight of one of the many televisions now surrounded by football fans completely oblivious to the show. Not being able to get close enough, I resorted to desperate measures. Along with many others I moved to the side of the pitch where I could look up and see into the executive boxes. In almost every box the television was on and the occupants were watching the shoot-out. I could just about make out what was going on, and the crowd provided a commentary by cheering or groaning as England or Germany scored.

By the time Stuart Pearce had his shot saved by the West German keeper, Illgner, The Stones had left the stage – they were also watching the shoot-out. The groan which greeted Chris Waddle's blaze over the bar was amazing. Everywhere you looked people were shaking their heads in disbelief, some appeared to be crying. Then, thank God, The Stones roared back on to the stage. It was the perfect antidote.

A truly weird evening. One which illustrated both the power of football and, more importantly, the power of the penalty shoot-out. It takes something extra special to stop The Rolling Stones, if only for a few minutes. However, this still hasn't answered the question: why do I think the penalty shoot-out is such a brilliant idea? More importantly, why was it introduced at all? And whose idea was it anyway?

To answer these questions, you need to understand the situation facing football in the late 1960s – a period when 'the beautiful game' was battling to improve its popular and commercial appeal. In particular, you first need to appreciate the problem of replays.

Replays

Many younger readers probably cannot remember the era of 'the replay': FA Cup Finals having to be replayed in the evening on the Wednesday or Thursday after the Final at Wembley; Cup matches all over the world, even World Cup qualifying matches, going to two or three replays, sometimes even more. The following examples, admittedly extreme, demonstrate the seriousness of the problem:

The record for the most number of replays in England is an FA Cup qualifying round in 1971. It went to five replays – a total of 660 minutes of playing time! Alvechurch finally beat Oxford City 1–0 on 22 November 1971, the first game having been played on 6 November. All except the first and last games went to extra-time. One journalist covering the fourth game reported that a comedian in the crowd had suggested an annual reunion for all those who had attended so far. Alvechurch had only four days' rest before the next round, which they lost 4–2 to Aldershot. It was their ninth game in eighteen days. Manchester United think they had it hard in 1997.

Replays had been causing problems for years. In the 1909 Scottish Cup Final between Rangers and Celtic, the outcome still had not been decided after two replays. At the end of the second replay, the frustrated and fairly intoxicated crowd hoped extra-time was to be played. The players also appeared confused, but when they left the field, clearly not intending to return, about 6000 people invaded the pitch. Many of them were convinced the two draws had been stage-managed by the two teams to produce more revenue from the replays. They tore up the goalposts, broke down fences, turnstiles and pay-boxes, and started a fire in the middle of the pitch, which they got burning with liberal sprinklings of whisky. Policemen, firemen and even ambulancemen were stoned by the mob, and the police resorted to throwing stones back at the rioters, eventually clearing the ground by 7 p.m., suffering fifty-four casualties in the process. The Cup was not awarded that year.

The Glasgow fans may have been suspicious about the two replays, but the fact was there was no provision in the Scottish Football Association Rules for extra-time. The game had to go to another replay.

One of the most extraordinary games took place just after the Second World War – an FA Cup replay between Stockport County and Doncaster Rovers on 30 March 1946. With the score at 2–2 after extra-time, the teams decided to play on until the next goal was scored. Nobody scored and the game was abandoned when it got dark – at 6.43 p.m. after 203 minutes of play! Some reports have supporters going home for tea and then coming back later to find the match still going. Doncaster won the second replay 4–0.

War-time conditions required Cup-ties to be completed at the first attempt. As a result at least one match took over three hours: on 14 April 1945, in the second round of the Football League North War Cup, Cardiff City and Bristol City played for 3 hours and 22 minutes before the deciding goal was scored.

Replays were also a problem for the players. Endless replays significantly increased the risk of serious injury. And they did not help much if you were involved in the latter stages of several competitions. The following example, ironically enough, comes from 1980, some ten years *after* the shoot-out was created:

Arsenal v Liverpool – the most protracted semi-final in the history of the FA Cup. Four games, and 420 minutes of football, played between 12 April and 1 May (nine days before the Final itself). Arsenal won through, but then had to play two League games before Wembley. Unsurprisingly, the Arsenal players were rather tired by the time the Final came around, which probably accounts for the fact they managed to lose to the football equivalent of Halley's Comet – a Trevor Brooking header. Worse was to follow. Four days later they travelled to the Heysel Stadium in Brussels for the European Cup Winners' Cup Final, losing on penalties to Valencia (see Appendix 1).

The Cup Winners' Cup Final was Arsenal's sixteenth game in 46 days, and they still hadn't finished. If Arsenal had won their last two League games they would have qualified for a UEFA Cup place but, sadly for them, they won only one. Arsenal had played seventy matches, reached two Cup Finals, and won absolutely nothing.

Replays were unacceptable to the authorities for another important reason: the United States of America. Football in the late 1960s was desperately trying to improve its popular and commercial image, not least because there was a real chance of cracking the most important market of all – the USA.

If you are trying to improve a sport's appeal and, in particular, make it more acceptable for the USA, you must do a number of things. You have to make it more user-friendly for television, for a start. You have to add a bit of showbiz: cheerleaders, marching bands, and rock music every time a goal is scored. Most of all, though, you have to guarantee a result on the day.

Americans don't do draws. 'Replay' is not a word which features in the American sporting vocabulary. For example, Americans cannot, and never will, understand cricket. Any sport where a match can last five days, where the players stop for lunch and tea, and where a draw is often considered a good result, was clearly devised by someone with a serious substance-abuse problem. The idea of a match in any sport going to five replays is completely outwith an American's comprehension, no matter how big a sports fan.

In the States it has long been the case that simply attending a football, baseball, basketball or hockey game is an expensive business. Most tickets are season tickets, owned by fanatical fans or corporate clients, who have shelled out big bucks for the right to watch their team in the flesh. American football seats are handed down through the family like heirlooms, and recently 'soccer' has become very similar. And when you have paid a lot of money just to be at a game (forget all the extras) you expect a great 'product'. People will not pay for a season ticket or, indeed, subscribe on a regular basis for pay-for-view television, if there is the possibility of a drawn game. You have to ensure a result.

FIFA were keen to 'crack' America, and were sensitive to the problems posed by replays, but it was not yet at the top of their list of priorities. They had bigger fish to fry: hooliganism, negative play, even worse, violent play, and falling attendance figures to mention just a few. Yet the world football family was growing at an extraordinary rate, and the time-bomb of fitting replays into an ever more crowded calendar was slowly ticking away. Pressure grew, particularly in relation to international matches, from spectators who had paid substantial sums in tickets and travelling expenses, and expected to see a result and a Cup presentation. No decision, and a future replay, brought only disappointment, anti-climax, some anger, and often an inability, financially, on the spectator's part to repeat the occasion.

Things were difficult then – imagine how it would be now if Cup matches all over the world still went to two or even three replays? Well, I suppose even more football on television for a start.

Compounding the problem, FIFA had powerful traditional and commercial interests to overcome. Many clubs, particularly at the domestic level, and particularly in the United Kingdom, had a vested interest in encouraging replays. There was no satellite television underwriting the profitability of the game to extraordinary levels. Football clubs made their money from packing as many people as possible into rundown and primitive grounds, and playing as many games as possible. The price of a ticket was relatively low, and the guiding economic theory was 'stack 'em high, sell 'em cheap'. And if you have to sell 'them' cheap you have to sell lots of them. The players and managers may have complained about too many matches but to the club owners a crowded season often meant profit or financial survival.

The Best-laid Plans . . .

So FIFA had a lot on its plate in 1969, and to complicate matters even further, there was also a World Cup coming up in Mexico in 1970 – a tournament FIFA was desperate to make a success.

It may come as a surprise to everyone in the UK brought up on the glory that was 1966 to learn that, outside England, the 1966 World Cup had provoked grave concern about the state of the game. Such is the power of the images from the Final that people tend to forget Pelé being kicked out of the tournament or the brutality and cynicism of the Argentinians. Well, many commentators were predicting the 1970 tournament would be the same – 'a festival', but of all the wrong things. As one contemporary journalist put it: 'Football as a world-wide spectator sport will receive a deadly blow because of too defensive football and, even more, because of unfair, rough and dirty play.'

He was not alone, and FIFA was well aware that the main topic of football conversations around the world seemed to be about a possible disaster in Mexico as a result of 'rough and vicious play'. FIFA's hope was that the tournament 'would be decided by skill and not by muscle', with a successful World Cup providing a much-needed breathing space in which the game's fundamental problems could be addressed. There certainly was no intention to decide on any major law changes before the 1970 World Cup. On 21 June 1969, the International Board minuted: 'The Board agreed with the views expressed by Sir Stanley Rous, FIFA President, that for a period of time no fundamental changes should be made in the Laws of the Game and that the Board should devote some of its time to discussing trend and developments in the game. A working party will be established to consider any minor changes that will be necessary, and to report to the next meeting of the Board.'

Unknown to Sir Stanley and his colleagues, eight days prior to their board meeting, the flip of a coin had already taken place which was, at the risk of sounding incredibly hammy and melodramatic, to change the face of football for ever.

Heads or Tails

Matches going to two or three replays were bad enough in domestic competitions, but international tournaments, be they club or country, could not simply go on, replay after replay after replay. At some point there had to be a resolution if the players couldn't sort it out on the field. Unfortunately, the mechanism used prior to 1970 was, to say the least, unsatisfactory.

Let's face it, drawing lots or tossing a coin to decide important Cup matches was never destined to be hugely popular: if you've paid good money to go and see a match, spent money on programmes and refreshments, watched, in the case of some matches we will come to in a minute, 300 minutes of football, and are then told the result of the game is going to be decided by the flip of a coin, which sometimes you can't even see . . . I don't think so.

Two captains flipping a coin or a coloured disc, or two club presidents drawing coloured cards from a hat, is no way to end a football match. Allowing it to take place in the referee's changing room, with the crowd waiting in the stadium to hear the result, is no way to treat supporters. Yet, prior to the penalty shoot-out, a number of important international and club matches, involving some of the most famous names in football, were decided this way – entirely by chance.

The first time lots were used to decide a World Cup match was in 1954. Spain and Turkey were still tied after three matches of their qualifying game and so they drew lots, with Turkey winning. In June 1968, in the European Championship semi-final, Italy went through against USSR on the toss of a coin after a 0–0 draw. Trivia alert: the coin used for the toss was a 1916 ten-franc piece belonging to the German referee, Herr Tschenscher.

Between 1955 and 1970 the toss of a coin/drawing of lots was used seven times in the European Cup to decide matches, two of which involved famous British clubs. Glasgow Rangers were one of five teams to win this way in the Cup Winners' Cup, beating Real Zaragoza in the semi-final in 1967. In the Fairs Cup, which subsequently became the UEFA Cup, drawing lots was used twelve times between 1964 and 1970.

When you read the match reports of these games, you realize what a godsend the penalty shoot-out must have seemed. We are talking here about teams such as AC Milan, Liverpool, Chelsea, Cologne, Barcelona and Roma, all going out of European competitions for no other reason than a good or a bad guess. Following are three examples, all of which would probably result in riots and serious loss of life if repeated today.

AC Milan v Chelsea

'CHELSEA DO IT ON TOSS,' screamed the *Daily Mirror* headline, announcing Chelsea's victory over AC Milan, which put them through to the quarter-finals of the Inter-Cities Fairs Cup in March 1966.

The match in the San Siro on 2 March 1966 was a play-off, the home and away legs having failed to produce a result. Ironically, the reason the game was being played in Milan as opposed to Chelsea was because Milan had won the toss of a coin to decide the venue for the play-off. It was the fifth time Milan had been involved in a toss-up that season – three to decide venue of play-off and one to decide a tie itself. They had won all of them, but this time it was not to be.

From all the accounts of the game, admittedly English,

it would have been a travesty if Chelsea had lost. Milan equalized with a goal in the last minute from a corner: 'a decision at which even the Milan fans jeered' (*Daily Express*). Three Chelsea players were still arguing with the referee when the corner was taken. The goal itself was dubious: 'Bonetti was obviously pushed off balance as outside-left Fortunato put the ball into the goal.' However, it stood and the game went to extra-time, but no more goals were scored. As the two teams left the field, exhausted, the Italian crowd, which had previously been hurling cushions on to the pitch in frustration, lit bonfires and fireworks to celebrate their team's escape equalizer.

So it was in the middle of something resembling Dante's Inferno that the referee, Herr Baumgartel from West Germany, had to wait for the reappearance of the two captains to decide the match by the toss of a coin.

First out was Cesare Maldini, current coach of the Italian national team. He then had to wait five minutes before Chelsea captain Ron 'Chopper' Harris returned, to a storm of derision from the crowd. Harris later told reporters he had been asking an interpreter what he should call. Harris joined the posse of officials and photographers in the centre-circle, and the referee motioned him to call. Harris said afterwards: 'It was a foreign coin with a head on one side and an eagle on the other. I decided on the head right away.'

The coin was spun into the smoky night air. The San Siro went silent for a second as the heads bent down to look at the coin, and then it erupted in a cacophony of boos and jeers. Harris had decided correctly, and went off on a mad dance of delight with his manager, Tommy Docherty. Chelsea were through.

Two years later, Harris experienced what Maldini must have felt when he called incorrectly, and Chelsea went out of the same tournament, losing to DWS Amsterdam. After two goalless draws, the second-round tie came down to the toss of a silver Dutch guilder in the referee's changing room at the Olympic Stadium in Amsterdam. This time Harris got it wrong: 'I called correctly for Chelsea when we tossed against Milan three years ago. This time it went against us. I called "Heads" just as I did in Milan, but this time the referee caught the coin, turned his hand over, and there it was: "tails".'

Benfica v Celtic – European Cup, 1969

In November 1969, Celtic were 3–0 up from the home leg of their European Cup quarter-final against Benfica. In the away leg, in the Stadium of Light in Lisbon, Celtic conceded two goals and then were party to one of the more bizarre passages in football's history.

Three minutes into injury-time, Benfica's substitute, Diamentino, scored the equalizer with a header. Instead of putting the ball back on the centre spot and then blowing for full-time, as he should have done, the referee, M. Van Ravens of Holland, picked up the ball and dashed off the field. No one knew whether the score was 3–3 or 3–2 to Celtic, and the confusion resulted in some ugly scenes in the players' tunnel.

It appears the ref had locked himself in his dressing room and had it guarded by two Portuguese policemen. Then the great Eusebio, who had scored one of Benfica's goals but had gone off at half-time, burst into the corridor and had a heated exchange with several of the Celtic players. The upshot of all this confusion was that the referee ordered thirty minutes of extra-time to be played. This ended goalless, and so the tie had to be decided by the toss of a coin.

Instead of calling the two captains to the centre spot, the referee again made for the sanctuary of his dressing room, leaving 80,000 fans with an agonizing wait for the result. What happened next, and why not one but two tosses of the coin were required, was later explained to reporters by Celtic's captain, Billy McNeill: 'I was there, Coluna [Benfica's captain] was there, the referee was there, and there were a few neutral observers. A lot of people were mystified why I had to make two correct calls when the coin was spun, but this is the reason: I guessed at the start of the game; Coluna guessed for ends when we began extra-time, and the Dutch referee announced when we were summoned to his presence that it was therefore my turn to guess again to see who should make the final guess that was going to put either Celtic or Benfica into the quarter-finals. He pointed out the two sides of his silver coin, flipped it into the air after I had said "Heads", down it came, and heads it was. So that meant I had to win two in a row. I decided to stick by "Heads", and up went the guilder again. This time the referee failed to catch it. It hit him on the foot, and bounced against the grey concrete wall of his little dressing room. It bounced from one wall to the other, rolled around the floor on its milled edge for what seemed an eternity, and then went twisting down.

'Before it had come to a complete stop I could see it was heads, and then the bedlam was let loose. The Celtic players knew by our shouts that we were through – but I hope I don't have to live through so much torture again in so short a space of time.'

This fiasco was bad enough, but if one match ever highlighted the need for change to this rule, then the European Cup tie between Liverpool and Cologne, which had taken place four years earlier in March 1965, was surely it.

Liverpool v Cologne – European Cup, 1965

The home and away legs were goalless, and so there was a replay at the neutral venue of Rotterdam. Ian St John and Roger Hunt put Liverpool 2–0 up, but the Germans converted two difficult chances to equalize. There were no more goals and so the game had to be decided by the toss of a coin or, in this case, the toss of a disc. Instead of a coin, the referee had a special disc. One side was red and the other white. The disc was spun into the air by the referee – if it came down red,

Liverpool went through; white, and Cologne would win. It was then the farce started.

I swear this is a true story. Ian St John later described his feelings as the toss took place in his book, *Boom at the Kop*:

> When the final whistle went at 2–2, and after extra-time it was the same, the stage was set for an incredible climax to a big match as you could wish to see. There were fifty-five thousand fans waiting in nervous silence for the toss of the red-and-white plastic disc. And the players, exhausted and keyed-up, hung around the centre of the pitch waiting for Referee Henri Schaut to flip it into the air.
>
> Before the match we had joked with big Ron [Yeats] that if it came to a toss-up we'd be all right. 'You're bound to win,' we told him in the dressing room. Because the truth is that Ron is often very lucky at the odd flutter on cards or horses.
>
> But now it had to be third time lucky. Because Ron had lost the toss at the start of the game . . . and at the start of extra-time . . . with the same plastic disc they were now using. Anyway, up flew the disc to decide which of us would meet Inter Milan in the semi-final. And down it came to the pitch. I didn't go near the toss-up. I couldn't stand the tension. Instead, I stood with Peter Thompson some distance away. I saw the disc go up and come down, saw none of the red jerseys jumping in jubilation and said, 'We've lost!' Then I stopped short and corrected myself: 'No, wait, they are tossing again.' Because, of course, the disc had landed on its *edge* in the mud.
>
> Up went the disc again, down it came once more – and up into the air leaped Ron Yeats with his long arms outstretched with joy. It had landed red-side up. I turned to Peter and said: 'We're through.'

They had played five hours of football, and the result came down to the consistency of the Rotterdam mud.

Nowadays, of course, this would not be a problem. Andy

Gray and the Sky TV virtual-reality replay gizmo would be able to determine the exact angle of incline of the disc and thus obviate the need for another disc-toss. However, Andy Gray was just a kid in 1965, and Sky just a twinkle in Rupert Murdoch's eye. Referee's everywhere were busy making themselves special plastic discs, and captains would spend hours practising their calling technique.

Some of you may be wondering about the interplay between drawing lots and tossing a coin. Prior to 1966, it seems it was basically up to the referee to choose, with the result that a variety of methods were used: drawing lots from a hat, tossing a coloured disc, or tossing a coin. Trivia alert: the rule governing the drawing of lots to decide a drawn game was formalized at the seventh meeting of FIFA's Referees' Committee held in Moscow on 9 and 10 September 1966. It became known officially as the 'Moscow Recommendation', and read as follows: 'The drawing of lots should be done by a toss of a coin; the referee should ask the visiting Captain to choose between Heads or Tails and indicate to the Home Captain whether he was Heads or Tails. The referee should then toss the coin. If a match were played on a neutral ground, the referee should decide which team should be "Heads" and which team "Tails", and after informing the Captains toss the coin.'

There was also a proposal, put forward in respect of matches played at a neutral venue, to have the referee organize a toss of the coin before the game started. This would decide who was going to be the home side for the purpose of any later coin-toss. So, you had to toss a coin to decide who would get to choose when you later tossed a coin to decide who won the game!

The flaw in this idea was clear: how did you choose who was 'heads' or 'tails' on the toss to decide who was the home side for the purpose of the later toss to decide who won the game – another coin toss? Spoofing? A game of 'scissors, rocks and paper'?

The Moscow Recommendation side-stepped this potential 'Catch-22'. However, it left itself open to an aggrieved losing captain thinking there was a fix when the referee told him he was a 'tail' and it came up 'heads'.

There was also confusion as to where the coin toss should take place – on the pitch or in the changing rooms? Can you imagine the 1966 World Cup Final being decided by the toss of a coin in the referee's changing room, while the Queen and 100,000 people waited outside? Whether you were talking about a coin-toss, a coloured-disc-toss, or the picking of pieces of card from a hat, this rule was an accident waiting to happen. Sure enough, the wheels came off in a World Cup qualifying match in 1969.

Problems in North Africa

On 13 June 1969, Morocco played Tunisia in the third match of their second-round qualifying tie. The first two games having been drawn, the third game was played at the neutral venue of Marseille. The score was 2–2 after extra-time and so the game went to the 'drawing of lots', which, pursuant to the Moscow Recommendation, meant the toss of a coin.

Morocco won the toss amidst much controversy. It should be noted here that the two countries were not exactly on friendly terms before the match. They had serious political differences, but that was not the main cause of the conflict. In 1962 Tunisia had lost on the drawing of lots to Morocco following a play-off in Palermo, Sicily. In 1968 the two countries had met again, this time in the qualifying round of the Olympics, and, you've guessed it, Morocco again won on the drawing of lots.

The Tunisian Association could not believe its team had lost a third time, and forwarded a written protest to FIFA about the way in which the 'coin was tossed'. It submitted photos and film sequences of the toss to support its claim of irregularities. An official investigation took place but found no evidence of double-headed coins or the like. The result stood, Morocco went through to the next round and ultimately became the first African nation to reach the finals themselves. However, the damage to the Moscow Recommendation had been done. The search for an alternative began, and it did not take long to find.

The Shoot-out Is Born

The August 1969 edition of *FIFA News* contained the following piece, written by Michael Almog of Tel Aviv, Israel. Mr Almog was a member of both the African Football Confederation Technical Committee and the Executive Committee of the Israel Football Association, of which he later became chairman. This is his article in full:

> It has been accepted until the present that the system used in official football tournaments to decide the winner, even if after extra-time the two teams are still equal, is tossing of a coin or drawing lots to qualify a team for the next round or even for the final tie.
>
> My opinion is that if the winner is decided by drawing of lots it is not a sportive way to win a competition. I propose that a competent committee, in the framework of FIFA, should decide to cancel this system for international tournaments (e.g. World Championships, Olympic Football Tournament, Continental Championships). If FIFA would cancel this system the Confederations will probably do so in their official tournaments and Cup tournaments of champion teams. The National Associations will be free to use which method they think fit.
>
> I propose to stop this way of deciding the winner by drawing of lots because it is immoral and even cruel, it is unfair to the

losing team and not honourable for the winner. Therefore, I propose that the matter be reconsidered very seriously and a decision reached as soon as possible.

One of the alternatives for the changing of this system could be that at the end of a match when, even after extra-time, the winner has still not been decided (if the competition is played by eliminating the loser), another match will be held at least 24 hours after this match, played according to the same system (extension of time). Even if then the winner is not decided, 5 penalty kicks will be taken by each team by different players (from the 11 who finished the match). If the winner is still not determined one penalty kick will be taken by each team until the winner is eventually decided.

I am not suggesting that this system is the best one, but I think it is better than the system of drawing lots because it is more sportive and more convincing for both sides participating in the competition.

This was not the first time a form of penalty shoot-out had been proposed as a replacement for drawing lots. It seems variants of the Almog proposal had been knocking around Europe for a number of years.

It was, however, the first real attempt to put the idea on the International Board's agenda – the mere fact that the article was published in *FIFA News* indicates that the FIFA hierarchy was taking the matter seriously. However, the shoot-out had some formidable opponents.

In a lecture given in September 1969, Sir Stanley Rous referred to some of the suggestions he regularly received on how to improve the game. Just as today, there was no shortage of reformers, and the ideas include many still being championed now. These are some of them:

- Bigger goals – higher and wider – to help poor marksmen (smaller goalkeepers would be just as effective!)

- A thirty-yard line across the field at either end, inside which most fouls occur, with the suggestion that each foul in the new area be penalized by a penalty kick. Those of you with good memories will recall this was suggested by the Scottish FA in 1894.
- Hockey-type corners, both short and long.
- Penalty shots and/or corners deciding drawn games after extra-time.
- Two referees.
- New methods of scoring points.
- No offside, or no offside at all free-kicks.
- Four-step law – this, in fact, has caused no difficulty in any part of the world, but some national associations are acting contrary to it by preventing goalkeepers from dribbling the ball.

Sir Stanley then told this story about the practice of drawing lots: 'Tossing a coin to decide a winner is unsatisfactory. On the whole I think the card system is preferable. Even this produces problems. In a recent Italy v Yugoslavia match in Naples, when no decision was reached in the second match, two identical cards were placed in a hat. Both presidents checked the cards to see that they were not marked or defaced in any way. The visiting team's card was drawn first. The home president immediately said, "But this is a Yugoslav hat." "No," said the Yugoslav, "Look, it was bought in Rome."'

The match he was referring to was actually the semi-final of the 1960 Olympics. The reference to 'identical cards' is a little confusing – what Sir Stanley meant was that the cards were the same type but different colours.

I have to confess, I can see little practical difference between tossing a coin and drawing lots from a hat, save that for the latter the referee would need a hat. I find it more interesting that, while by this stage Sir Stanley was aware of the shoot-out idea, he was not suggesting the replacement of the Moscow

Recommendation but rather an update of it. His view did not prevail.

The reason it did not prevail was Mr Koe Ewe Teik of Malaysia. Mr Teik was a senior member of FIFA's Referees' Committee, and it was he who made Almog's idea become reality.

Teik ensured the next meeting of FIFA's Referees' Committee, held on 14 and 15 February 1970, considered a proposal to review the Moscow Recommendation in the context of the penalty shoot-out as one of a number of potential alternatives. On 10 February 1970, he wrote to his fellow members setting out the basis of possible shoot-out rules, should the Committee decide to recommend change. This is the relevant part of his letter:

> If the meeting decides to recommend the taking of five penalty kicks for the consideration of the International Board, I suggest that the proposal be worded as given below:
>
> **Penalty Kicks**
>
> Penalty kicks to decide the winning team shall be taken in the following manner:
>
> 1. The referee shall choose the goal at which all the penalty kicks shall be taken.
> 2. The captains shall toss and the winning team shall first take five successive penalty kicks.
> 3. Each kick shall be taken by a different player of the same team selected from those already in the team at the end of the extension time.
> 4. If, after the five kicks, the number of goals scored be the same, the penalty kicks shall be continued by a different player, each taking a penalty kick alternately between the two teams until the result is decisive.

5. The goalkeeper may be changed by any other player already in the field, at any time during the process of the penalty kicks.

The Almog/Teik idea was approved as an option to be put forward to the 'Working Party on Trends in Modern Football', which was considering proposals to be placed before the next meeting of the International Board. The Working Party was also asked to consider the number of corners won by each team, together with drawing lots, although Sir Stanley Rous' recommendation to dispense with the tossing of a coin and instead pick pieces of a paper from a hat had become the preferred method (without the penalty shoot-out a hat would now be an obligatory part of a referee's equipment).

There are no detailed minutes of the discussion on this issue by the International Board Meeting held on 27 June 1970 at the Caledonian Hotel, Inverness, Scotland. However, the shoot-out proposal was approved, although the idea of one team taking all its penalties in one go was changed, and replaced by the system of alternate penalties we know today. More importantly, the Board made clear the idea was nothing more than a 'recommendation to the individual Committee of Competition'. In other words, you didn't have to introduce it if you didn't want to. The decision was too late for the Mexico World Cup, the rules governing the latter stages of which provided for the resolution of drawn matches by the drawing of names from a hat.

Kicks from the Penalty Mark

The shoot-out law as devised in the space of twelve months in 1969–70 has changed little to the present day. It is probably very familiar to most of us, but here is a summary of the key provisions currently in force:

- The goal at which all penalty kicks are taken is chosen by the referee.
- A coin-toss determines which team kicks first. There is no choice in the matter – win the toss and you have to take the first kick.
- Each team takes five kicks – the kicks are taken alternately.
- If, before both teams have taken five kicks, one has scored more goals than the other could score, even if it were to complete its five kicks, no more kicks are taken.
- Only players who are on the field at the end of the match, i.e., at the end of extra-time, are eligible to take part in the shoot-out.
- The team which scores the greater number of goals is deemed the winner, but the game is recorded as a draw with an additional notation that that the winner was decided on penalty kicks.
- If, after five kicks are completed, both teams have scored the same number of goals, the procedure continues until one team has scored one goal more than the other after both have taken an equal number of kicks.

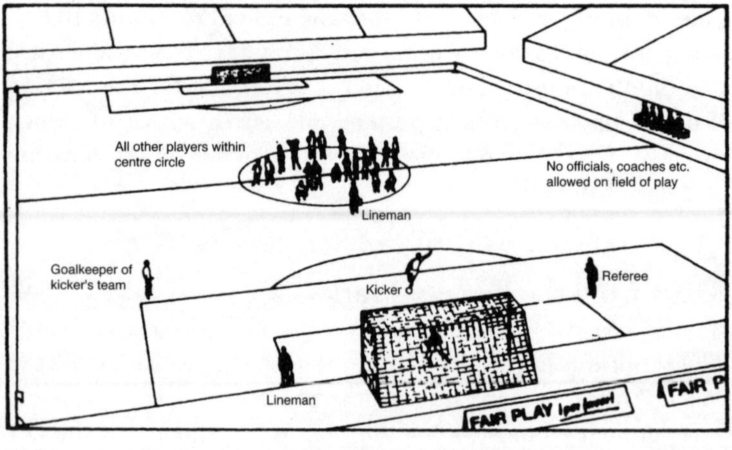

Positions at the shoot-out

- No player may take a second kick until all eligible teammates have had their turn.
- If the goalkeeper is injured during the shoot-out, he may be replaced by a team-mate who is already on the field, or by a substitute, provided his team has not already made use of the maximum number of substitutes permitted by the rules.
- Other than the player taking the kick and the opposing goalkeeper, all players must remain within the centre-circle while the shoot-out is in progress.
- The goalkeeper who is waiting for his turn to save must remain in the field of play but outside the penalty area, at least 10 yards from the penalty spot, and further than 18 yards from the goal-line.
- Except as expressly superseded by the above rules, all the Laws of the Game apply throughout a shoot-out contest.

I thought I knew the procedure pretty well, but there are a few little wrinkles hidden away in the 'Check-list for Referees', issued by FIFA, which I doubt many people are aware of. The reality is that they will probably never have any practical impact, but I mention them because they show that captains may still have to rely on their coin-tossing skills, albeit in extreme circumstances. It's also great trivia:

- If, at the taking of penalty kicks from the penalty mark, the light fails badly and the kicks cannot therefore be completed, the result shall be decided by the tossing of a coin or the drawing of lots.
- If the lights fail at a stadium after extra-time but before the taking of kicks from the penalty mark, and if they cannot be repaired in a reasonable time, the referee shall decide the match by tossing a coin or drawing lots.
- If at the end of the match some players leave the field of play and fail to return for the taking of kicks from the penalty mark, and are not injured, the referee will not allow the kicks

to be taken and will report the matter to the responsible authorities.

- If kicks from the penalty mark cannot be taken because of riots or similar reasons, the referee shall wait a reasonable time, but if matters do not improve the result shall be decided by tossing a coin or drawing lots.
- If a situation arises where the winner of a match must be determined by tossing a coin or by drawing lots, this procedure should be conducted immediately after the match by the referee, but if for some reason this is not done, it may be carried out later by the competition organizer.
- If the captains of both teams mutually agree not to take kicks from the penalty-mark to determine the winner of the match, despite the fact that this is stipulated in the regulations of the competition, the referee must make a report to the appropriate competition authorities explaining what happened.

The last provision may seem strange, but it has recently been invoked (more in Chapter 4).

One final thing to remember is that you should never call the shoot-out process 'Penalties'. This really offends the purists, and particularly referees, because, as they quite rightly point out, these are not penalties – no foul has been committed or penalty awarded. The 'penalties' are simply kicks taken from the penalty mark to resolve a drawn match, which is why the game itself is always officially recorded as a draw. However, as it is far too time consuming to type out 'kicks from the penalty mark' each time, I propose, with all apologies to my referee friends, to use the word 'penalties'.

For or Against

Almog and Teik's solution guaranteed a result, involved the players, an element of skill, and was clearly going to be dramatic. It relied on some actual football, albeit in an abbreviated form. At the very, very least, it was better than drawing pieces of coloured paper from a hat, or tossing coins. Nevertheless, the shoot-out quickly gained powerful critics. The rise and, I hope, temporary fall of the penalty shoot-out are documented in the next chapter.

Careers Advisory Service

The historical details in this chapter are derived from some painstaking and laborious research through the FIFA archives in Zurich. Yes, for the sake of literary integrity I had to spend three days in Zurich in June 1997, at the kind invitation of Keith Cooper and Marius Schneider of FIFA's Communications Division. It's a hard life.

One thing that struck me quite forcibly while I was there was: how come my careers adviser at school never mentioned a job with FIFA as a possible career path?

FIFA's offices are modern, spacious and elegant, situated in a leafy Zurich suburb, with a phenomenal view over the lake and the city itself. The organization is staffed by some of the nicest people you could wish to meet – courteous, interesting and multi-lingual. The interchange between languages was sometimes so fast I could have sworn they'd made up a new language all of their own.

Therein lies the problem. My careers adviser did not have a FIFA brochure when I went to see him because to work at FIFA you are required to speak, read and write other languages. This effectively rules out 99.9 per cent of the British population. Mind you, I think I might have concentrated a little harder in my French and German lessons if someone had told me it might help me get a job where you are paid to be involved with football at the highest level, and, wait for it, every four years you are paid to attend the World Cup!

All you teenagers out there: work hard on your foreign languages and then give your careers officer serious grief about a job in football administration. With football continuing to take over the world, sporting and otherwise, football administration is already becoming the next Civil Service, BBC or merchant-banking career. You heard it here first.

4 – History of the Shoot-out

The First Shoot-out

The first penalty shoot-out in a senior competitive football match took place in the United Kingdom on 5 August 1970 – barely a month after the International Board's approval. Manchester United were the first winners, defeating Hull City 4–3 on penalties in the semi-final of the Watney Cup. Trivia alert: the first player to score in a shoot-out was George Best – the greatest football player ever.

I cannot tell you how happy I was when I read the match report of the first senior penalty shoot-out. George Best is my favourite player of all time. Readers may not agree with the statement that he was the greatest player ever, but I feel comforted that my opinion is shared by the only other player with a claim to the title – Pelé. If Pelé believes Best is the most talented player he has ever seen, that's good enough for me.

Unfortunately for this book, Best was not a regular penalty taker. It seemed I would have to write it without any reference to my hero. Then I discovered the Watney Cup story. Even better, I found a book Best had written in 1968 called *Best of Both Worlds* – clearly ghost-written, but still a fascinating account of Best's involvement in the famous year culminating in United's European Cup victory over Benfica at Wembley. The final chapter is called, naturally enough, 'The Future', and in it, amongst other things, Best calls for the introduction of a European Super League (years ahead of his time). However, he also indulges in a little dream sequence, which, without any apology, I repeat in full below:

> I am not dreaming as I look forward to a Manchester United Cup Final within a very few seasons . . . I see us get a couple of goals and then George Best will produce the greatest show of individual talent ever seen on a football field. I know what I shall do.
>
> As the Manchester United thousands are singing their songs of praise, victory seems inevitable. The Cup is going back to Manchester. Only the last twenty minutes remain, and with United in such superb and invincible form it is time to show off.
>
> A long kick-out from goalkeeper Alex Stepney comes ballooning down the field towards me and I move in to trap it – against the turf with my backside. Imagine the roar that rends the air at this spectacular show of virtuosity. The cheek of it; the rank impudence of a player so much in control that he can bring a ball under his spell by sitting on it as it hits the deck after a high-flying 75-yard punt from the goal.
>
> Quickly, I am up with the ball, laying it off to a colleague, and Denis Law runs across with a wagging finger to tell me: 'Stop taking the mickey.'
>
> But I haven't finished. This is Wembley . . . the Queen is here . . . and the television cameras . . . and millions of people throughout the country are watching the match in their own front parlours. There are more tricks for the photographers and headline writers. I sweep past the left flank of the opposing defence, bouncing the ball on my thighs and never letting it touch the ground.
>
> In the dying minutes we are awarded a penalty and I am called upon to take it. The act is building up into a climax. The

gaping 100,000 crowd wonder what the showman will do this time. Back-heel it in? Merely pass to a colleague?

No. I shall call to the goalkeeper as he takes up his position like a nervous cat. I shall say: 'It's going in off the crossbar.' And it does.

The crowd is in ecstasies. The show of magic has them almost delirious. It is preposterous that anyone should dare to attempt such outrageous tricks at Wembley. But the best is yet to come. The final rite is reserved for the closing minutes, for a stunt that would be regarded as fantastic even in the circus ring.

The crowd is ready for more goals. The excitement has them baying crazily for more of this compulsive entertainment, when a centre flies across the face of the opposition goal. It's mine and it's at headable height. Denying all the known laws of balance and past-practice I fly into a handstand and volley the ball into the foot of the net with my feet.

I know, absolutely nothing to do with shoot-outs, but you just know he could probably have done the handstand trick.

Back to the Watney Cup, a competition which has always seemed happy to experiment with new approaches to the game. It quickly embraced the shoot-out, which appeared to go down well with everyone except Hull City. Most commentators certainly appear to have welcomed the innovation. The *Daily Telegraph* said: 'This was the first time this method of settling a match had been used at senior level in England and it must be rated a resounding success. The suspense, as five players from each side fired alternately, was almost intolerable.'

The *Daily Mail*'s Brian Taylor wrote 'The penalty-taking session which settled this pulsating game was one of the most exciting and dramatic features I have ever seen on a soccer field.'

The *Daily Mirror* called it a 'tremendous hit'.

The shoot-out itself was a classic. No scriptwriter could have dreamed that the first penalty shoot-out at senior level would involve a set of five players for one team consisting of: George Best, Brian Kidd, Bobby Charlton, Denis Law and Willie Morgan (plus Alex Stepney in goal).

George Best stepped up first for United and scored with a low shot to the keeper's right. Terry Neil scored for Hull, and then followed goals for Kidd, Butler, Charlton and Simpkin, making it 3–3. Then— Trivia alert: Denis Law, who had headed United's equalizer during normal time, became the first player in senior competitive football to miss a kick in a shoot-out, Hull's keeper, McKechnie, diving to save to his right. Ken Wagstaff took the fourth kick for Hull, and missed. Willie Morgan calmly put his kick away, and so it was up to McKechnie to keep Hull in the competition.

Watney Cup Soccer

PENALTY-KICKING COMPETITION SEES UNITED THROUGH

By ROBERT OXBY

Hull .... 1 Manchester U. 1
(*after extra time: United win on penalties* 4-3)

HISTORY was made at Boothferry Park last night when Manchester United, held to a 1-1 draw after extra time, won their way into the Watney Cup final at Derby on Saturday following a penalty competition.

This was the first time this method of settling a match had been used at senior level in England and it must be rated a resounding success. The suspense, as five players from each side fired alternately was almost intolerable.

DERBY THROUGH

Derby County, keeping a close control of play, deservedly beat Sheffield United in the other Watney Cup semi-final

Brian Kidd (right), the Manchester United inside-left, gets in a shot as Hull City defenders close in, but his shot is deflected for a corner by the Hull goalkeeper, Ian McKechnie.

Report of the first senior professional shoot-out.
The Daily Telegraph, *6 August 1970*

The decision to entrust the keeper with the vital kick was not as strange as it may seem. In a penalty knock-out tournament the previous close-season, McKechnie had reached the final with his team-mate, Ian Butler. Unfortunately for Hull, it was not to be. McKechnie's fierce left-foot shot was tipped on to the bar and over by Alex Stepney (or simply went over the bar, depending on the report you read) and United went through to the Final against Derby, which they won.

It was to be another twelve years before the shoot-out reared its head in the holiest of holies – the FA Cup. A key element of the decision by the International Board to approve its introduction was the fact that it was discretionary. Not only could individual associations and competition organizers choose whether they wanted it at all, if so, they could choose at what stage in the competition it kicked in.

FIFA and UEFA adopted it immediately, but in different measures. It soon became part of all the European Cup competitions but, partly because of the way the competitions were organized (round robins rather than pure knock-out), it was only relevant for the Final and 3rd/4th play-offs in the 1974 and 1978 World Cups, and was not required in any event.

It was of much more immediate relevance to the European Championships, which in those days had a qualifying tournament over two years, leading straight into the quarter-finals. The penalty shoot-out finally arrived in the big time, with a bang, in the 1976 Championship in Yugoslavia.

1976 European Championship Final – Czechoslovakia v West Germany

The first penalty shoot-out to decide a major international competition remains unique for another reason. It is the only time Germany have lost a penalty shoot-out. West Germany were the most successful national team of the 1970s, beating the 'total footballers' of Holland in the 1974 World Cup Final, and reaching three European Championship Finals in a row. However, by 1976 they were in (relative) decline. I stress the 'relative' – they still made the final of the '76 European

Championship; it's just that they weren't favourites. Czechoslovakia had beaten England, the USSR and Holland to get to the Final. Germany's progress had been less impressive, but they'd got there all the same. However, by half-time the Czechs led 2–0 and were looking comfortable.

As we have seen over the years – Hungary in 1954, England 1966, Holland 1974, Argentina 1986 – the Germans have made the last-minute escape an art form, and they did it again this time, Bernd Holzenbein heading in a last-minute corner to force extra-time. No goals in extra-time meant penalties would decide a major international championship for the first time.

The first seven penalties went in: Masny, Nehoda, Ondrus and Jurkemik scored for Czechoslovakia; Bonhof, Flohe and Bongartz for Germany. So the score was 4–3 on penalties when Uli Hoeness strode forward for Germany.

Hoeness was one of the unsung heroes of the successful Bayern Munich and West German teams of the 1970s, and had scored goals in many important matches. However, he was not a recognized penalty taker – he'd missed one in the 1974 World Cup. He wasn't particularly keen to take this one but was, apparently, persuaded to do so by Franz Beckenbauer. This is Hoeness' recollection of what happened next: 'I decided to give him a heavy shot, to try to put it in one corner. The ball was over the wall and I think they found him now a year ago. They had a war and the stadium was destroyed and they found the ball.'

Translation: he blasted it over the bar.

All Antonin Panenka had to do was score to win the tournament, and he came up with the most extraordinary penalty – a strange little chip down the middle of the goal, while the keeper dived to his left. Czechoslovakia won the Championship and Hoeness didn't play for West Germany again.

The only other European Championship shoot-out of note until Euro '96 occurred in the Denmark v Holland semi-final in 1992. Peter Schmeichel saved Van Basten's second kick and no one else failed, so Kim Christofte scored the penalty that put Denmark into the Final.

The World Cup

As we have already seen, the new rule was too late for the 1970 World Cup. If Brazil and Italy had drawn in Mexico City instead of producing one of the greatest games of all time, there would have been extra-time, a replay, extra-time and then the drawing of lots.

The next two World Cups, in 1974 and 1978, did not have a knock-out match until the Final itself. A shoot-out would have resulted if the Finals had remained tied after extra-time, a replay and another period of extra-time, but in neither was it required. It was not until the 1982 tournament that the World Cup saw a penalty shoot-out.

Not many people remember the three qualifying matches decided by a shoot-out: Nigeria beat Tunisia (who probably wanted to go back to coin-tossing), Morocco beat Zambia, and China beat Hong Kong. But who can ever forget the incredible semi-final between France and West Germany. Possibly the most exciting and controversial World Cup match of all time, settled by a shoot-out which started at midnight!

1982 World Cup Semi-final – France v West Germany

1982. The Sánchez Pizjuán Stadium in Seville, Spain. France have just drawn 1–1 with West Germany in regulation time. The Royal Oak public house in Ealing, West London. I am watching the match in my local with a crowd of Frenchmen. For most of regulation time the score is 1–1 and the game has been one long, drunken rendition of La Marseillaise. Harald Schumacher, the German keeper, commits a foul on Patrick Battiston for which he should be convicted of grievous bodily harm. My new French friends completely lose it. I fear for the safety of the television, even more so when, unbelievably, after France score twice in the first ten minutes of extra-time the Germans claw their way back into the match; Karl-Heinz Rummenigge, who was injured but on the bench, coming on and scoring. Then, with the French tiring rapidly, Klaus Fischer scored the equalizer with twelve minutes to go. I've never heard a pub go so quiet so quickly. The game went to penalties – the first time a World Cup finals match would be decided this way.

I think most neutral supporters were behind France before the Schumacher assault on Battiston. The style of Platini, Alain Giresse and Jean Tigana had certainly captivated me. I was by now drinking red wine and attempting to speak to the French guys in a quite extraordinary accent. None of us could believe they'd thrown away a two-goal lead but, Schumacher apart, you had to admire the Germans. They simply didn't know when they were beaten. Moreover, they were about to prove they had learnt their lesson from 1976. The German domination of *Elfmetershießen* was about to begin.

It was nearly midnight when the first penalty was taken but it was still very hot in Seville. Giresse scored, as did Kaltz for Germany. Rocheteau gave the disgraced Schumacher no chance and then, unbelievably, Stielike missed the goal completely.

Surely the French wouldn't let it slip now. But Didier Six, their flamboyant winger, had his saved by Schumacher. Pierre Littbarski levelled the scores and Platini and Rummenigge both scored. Now it was sudden death.

Bossis was the first up for France (he was not a regular penalty taker and looked in shock as he approached the ball). He put it to the right and Schumacher dived to the left. The only problem was Bossis' shot missed the goal by some little distance.

At least Schumacher didn't save it – that would have been too much to bear, given he should not have been on the pitch. Sadly for France, Hrubesch kept his nerve and possibly the best French team ever had thrown away a golden opportunity to reach the World Cup Final.

Platini left the field in tears. However, four years later he was to feel what it was like to win a shoot-out: a record which makes him admirably qualified to discern whether they work (see Chapter 5).

1986 World Cup Quarter-final – Brazil v France

When Michel Platini popped up at the far post to score five minutes from half-time, it was the first goal Brazil had conceded in the 1986 World Cup finals. This, the quarter-final, was their fifth match, and Brazil were looking good, having gone ahead through a Careca goal.

Then Platini equalized – it was his last goal for France – and suddenly it was anyone's game. Even then Brazil had chances to win it in normal time. First Careca hit the bar, then Branco was brought down by goalkeeper Joel Bats: penalty.

The great Zico had been on the field for less than two minutes. Rather spookily, in the 1978 finals he had come on as a substitute, against Peru, and within two minutes had scored from the penalty spot. No prizes, then, for guessing who grabbed the ball to take the kick which would probably send Brazil into the semi-finals.

He missed it. Zico hit it too close to Bats, the game went to extra-time and France won the penalty shoot-out 4–3. The equally great Socrates missed Brazil's first shot. Zico didn't play for Brazil again, and, sadly for the French, they failed to play anywhere near to their potential and lost to West Germany in the semi-final.

1990 World Cup Semi-final – England v West Germany

I was tempted not to write anything about this shoot-out – everything that could possibly be written has already been written, and by far better writers than me. But then I thought, 'What the hell – it's my book.' So, here goes.

That the game had to be decided by penalties was actually a miracle in itself, as the British press had written-off England completely. Mind you, this was understandable given the way the two teams had reached the semi-finals. West Germany had cruised through the early rounds, England had drawn with Holland and Eire, scraped past Egypt 1–0, won in the last minute of extra-time against a Belgian team that had hit the post twice, and then needed two penalties to beat Cameroon 3–2.

However, as we all know, the match itself was really competitive. The German goal was a complete fluke – Andy Brehme's free-kick hitting Paul Parker and looping over a helpless Shilton. Lineker equalized (coolness under pressure personified) and Buchwald and Waddle hit the post in extra-time.

Nor were England uncompetitive in the shoot-out. The first three penalty takers (Lineker, Beardsley, Platt) all scored easily. But so did the Germans. Shilton went the right way every time, but Brehme (whose penalty he'd saved in a 1985 friendly), Matthäus and Riedle all scored. Next up for England: the fierce left foot of Stuart Pearce. The best saved till next to last; so it seemed.

Pearce hit it typically hard, much too straight. Bodo Illgner went the wrong way but saved with his legs. Olaf Thon made it 4–3 although Shilts again guessed right. Waddle had to score to keep England in it.

The long legs shambled up, the ball went over the bar, England were out. In each of their last three matches, West

Germany scored only one goal: two penalties and (in a match decided on penalties) that huge deflection off Parker. Someone's *Namen* was on the cup, all right.

David Platt later said: 'Unfortunately for England, the Germans were in their element. Beckenbauer confirmed afterwards that they had been practising penalties, even though they had not looked remotely like needing them. England had not been practising, but even so, Shilton went the right way every time, the penalties were just too good.'

Stuart Pearce in a happier penalty shoot-out, against Spain during Euro '96 (Allsport)

European Tournaments

Shoot-outs became a regular feature of European club competition almost before the ink was dry on the IFAB resolution approving it. Stand by for some serious trivia:

- The first British teams to participate in a shoot-out were Aberdeen and Newcastle.
- In 1972, Glasgow Rangers won the European Cup-Winners' Cup despite being beaten in a penalty shoot-out in the second round. Rangers won the tie on away goals, but the referee didn't realize and so allowed the shoot-out to go ahead – which Sporting Lisbon duly won. The ref's decision was subsequently revoked and Rangers went on to win the 'Battle of Barcelona'.
- Ironically, Celtic were one of the first British teams to lose a shoot-out, no doubt prompting loud protests from Parkhead for the reintroduction of the coin-toss. Mind you, if ever a tie deserved to be decided by the toss of a coin, Celtic's European Cup semi-final against Internazionale in 1972 was probably it. Two goalless draws followed by thirty minutes of dire and scoreless extra-time. This time, however, the finalist would be decided by penalties.

John 'Dixie' Deans, the first man ever to score a hat-trick in the Final of both Scottish Cup competitions, took Celtic's first penalty . . . and blasted it over the bar. The other nine penalties were converted and Inter went through. Jock Stein, the Celtic manager, made a number of comments after the game, the only printable one being: 'We don't consider we lost on football, but to a circus turn.'

1980 European Cup-Winners' Cup Final – Arsenal v Valencia

By the time Arsenal reached the 1980 European Cup-Winners' Cup Final, they were an understandably tired team. They'd just lost to West Ham in the FA Cup Final. Not ideal preparation to face a Valencia team featuring the star of the 1978 World Cup Final, Argentinian Mario Kempes.

Arsenal had a pretty good team of their own: Liam Brady, Graham Rix, Frank Stapleton and Alan Sunderland were no slouches, but Valencia's defence, marshalled by the 19-year-old Tendillo, kept them out. There were no goals, even after extra-time, and so penalties would decide the match for the first time in any European club Final.

Mario Kempes took the first for Valencia and completed a miserable night by hitting a weak shot too close to Pat Jennings, who saved easily. Arsenal were nearly there, if they could only hold their nerve.

Sadly, it was not to be. Of all people, Liam Brady missed the first, putting it too near to Carlos Pereira, the Valencia keeper. Everyone then scored, so Valencia led 5–4 on penalties when Graham Rix stepped up. He had to score.

Rix was nearly as good with his left foot as Brady, but this was pressure of an unbelievable magnitude. His placement of the ball and run-up revealed the tension he was feeling and he hit much the same kind of shot as Kempes and Brady. Pereira saved again and Valencia won their first European trophy in nineteen years. Ironically, the three players who missed were probably the most gifted on the field and, not that it signifies anything, they were all left-footed.

Of the 41 European Cup Finals 5 have now been decided by a penalty shoot-out.

1984 European Cup Final

The final between Liverpool and Roma was held at Roma's home ground, the Olympic Stadium in Rome. With the game tied 1–1 after extra-time, the stage was set for the first penalty shoot-out in the twenty-eight-year history of the European Cup. It was held at the Italian fans' end of the stadium.

Phil Neal was a great penalty expert, and you would have expected him to lead off for Liverpool. Instead, Steve Nicol strode forward, and promptly blazed the ball over the bar. Di Bartolomei scored for Roma, placing the ball gently in the middle of the goal as Bruce Grobbelaar dived to one side. Neal scored with ease and then Conti shot even higher over the top than Nicol had done. Souness and Righetti both scored, as did Rush.

Graziani then stepped forward, to be greeted by the now famous 'wobbly jelly' impersonation from Grobbelaar. What real effect the play-acting had only Graziani can tell, but he chose to blast his shot and beat Grobbelaar completely. Unfortunately for him, the ball clipped the crossbar and went over.

It all depended on Alan Kennedy and he coolly placed the ball just inside the post: 'I was really confident. I took a penalty in training and put it in the same spot. Just like that.'

UEFA Cup Final, 1988

In the UEFA Cup Final of 1988, Bayer Leverkusen produced one of the great European comebacks. Trailing 3–0 from the first leg against Español, they were held goalless at half-time and seemed to have no chance.

Then the Brazilian Tita scored after 56 minutes, the East German Falko Gotz made it 2–0, and the Korean Cha Bum Kun 3–0 with nine minutes left. There were no goals in extra-time.

In the shoot-out, Ralf Falenmayer missed Bayer's first kick, but Santiago Urkiaga and Manuel Zuniga missed for Español, and, finally, with Rudi Vollborn waving his arms about on the line, Sebastian Losada completed the downfall (he'd scored twice in the first leg) by missing the decider. It was the first trophy Bayer had won in their eighty-four-year existence, and the only European Final either club's ever reached.

The FA Cup

The shoot-out was only introduced into the FA Cup in 1991–92, and the reason for its introduction had nothing to do with football and everything to do with crowd control. The catalyst was a request from the Association of Chief Police Officers for there to be a minimum of nine days between a Cup tie and a replay. This request had been prompted by the chaos caused by the Arsenal–Leeds match the previous year, which had gone to replays. The police request meant there could be no replay on the traditional Tuesday or Wednesday after the Saturday match, and so the FA reluctantly conceded.

Trivia alert: Scunthorpe were the first team to lose a penalty shoot-out in the FA Cup, losing to Rotherham 7–6 in November 1991. Scunthorpe's manager, Bill Green, was understandably disappointed: 'The beauty of the FA Cup has always been the David and Goliath aspect of it – the minnows stretching the big boys over two or three matches. The Cup is in danger of losing that magic after 120 years.'

What Green failed to say, reasonably enough given his team had just lost, was that penalty shoot-outs also gave the Davids a somewhat better chance of beating the Goliaths. The first Goliath to go was Newcastle, but the biggest shock of all came when Manchester United were beaten by Southampton in the fourth round. The shoot-out was no respecter of reputations. United were the Cup holders, and became the first Division One side to exit the Cup on penalties.

Following a goalless draw at The Dell, United quickly went 2–0 down at Old Trafford, courtesy of goals by Stuart Gray and Alan Shearer. Brian McClair got the equalizer a minute into injury-time, and United felt they had won the match in extra-time when Bryan Robson's header was shown on the television to have crossed the line. Sadly, for United, the referee wasn't refereeing the game from his front room and didn't allow the goal. Penalties followed, and Neil Webb and

Ryan Giggs (then only 18 years old) missed for United. Southampton scored all four of the penalties they had to take and didn't even need to call on the services of their expert penalty taker, Matt Le Tissier.

Man United's exit may have been the biggest shock caused by the new system, but the biggest debate was provoked by the defeat on penalties of Portsmouth in the semi-final against Liverpool.

The FA had, in fact, hoped to avoid using penalties at the semi-final stage of the tournament, but logistical problems made this impossible. The replay would normally have been held on 8 April, the Wednesday after the first game, but the West Midlands police asked for it to be put back to 13 April because of the General Election being held on 9 April. With Easter the following weekend and then England matches, the first free week for a second replay would have been only seven days before the Final.

The shoot-out defeat was made all the worse because Portsmouth had been just three minutes from Wembley in the first game at Highbury – denied by a Ronnie Whelan equalizer, following up a great free-kick from John Barnes.

Pompey also came close to winning the replay, but in the end succumbed 3–1 in the shoot-out. Kuhl, Berseford and Neill missed for Portsmouth while Barnes, Rush and Dean Saunders converted their penalties and put Liverpool in the Final (in which they beat Sunderland).

Jim Smith, then Pompey's manager (now of Derby County), accused penalties of 'trivializing' the Cup, and Ronnie Moran, Liverpool's caretaker manager, concurred: 'It is certainly a cruel way to go out of the competition. I know that if we had lost on penalties I would have been choked.'

Ian Rush perhaps summed it up best when he said after the victory: 'It is great when you win on penalties but it is a horrible way to lose.'

Graham Kelly, the FA's Chief Executive, was at that time on

FIFA's Task Force 2000 committee, a committee set up to canvass views on all aspects of the game's development. Kelly was aware of an alternative put forward by Michel Platini for the game to continue until a goal was scored. But, as Kelly pointed out at the time, policing and transport concerns made this idea unworkable: 'Portsmouth and Liverpool looked as though they might never score. They could have missed the last bus home.'

And it was in the FA Cup that Chris Waddle took his first spot kick after that miss in the 1990 World Cup. He surprised few people by missing it, and Sheffield Wednesday lost the shoot-out, in a fourth-round replay in 1994–95, to Wolves.

The Last One Out Please Turn off the Lights: Worst Shoot-outs

To be fair, penalty shoot-outs don't always work as planned. In 1975, in the Asia Cup semi-final between North Korea and Hong Kong, the game finished 2–2 after full-time and 3–3 after extra-time. The penalty shoot-out which followed went to 28 penalties, notwithstanding that 'sudden death' kicked in at the 11th penalty. North Korea eventually won.

There was also a 28-penalty shoot-out during a match between Aldershot and Fulham in 1987. Aldershot eventually won. And in a Marlow v Littlehampton fixture in the FA Amateur Cup in September '97, Marlow keeper Jamie Jackson hit the winning penalty after all twenty outfield players had scored. Littlehampton keeper Mark Howells missed.

In an early season tournament in South Africa in 1997, both semi-finals went to penalties, as did the Final between Orlando Pirates and Kaizers Chiefs. It took 30 penalties to decide the match – the Pirates eventually winning.

Amazingly, this is not the record for the longest shoot-out. That dubious honour goes to two teams in the Costa Rican

Primera Division, in a game played in January 1997. Shoot-outs are very common in Costa Rica, because when a League game is drawn a penalty shoot-out contest is immediately held, with the winner earning an extra point. At the game between Asociacion Deportiva and Turrialba Futbol Club, held in the National Stadium, the score after full-time was 0–0. Any spectator who remained behind to experience the excitement and drama of the shoot-out must have been sadly disappointed. It took 38 penalties to settle the contest, Turrialba winning the one extra point.

1990–94: The 'Beautiful Game' Gets a Make-over

Following the 1990 World Cup fiasco and the 1994 World Cup the general consensus seemed to be the 'beautiful game' had become beautiful again, and attacking football had triumphed. FIFA took the credit – they had introduced three points for a win in the first round, outlawed the tackle from behind, insisted on a liberal interpretation of the offside law, forced injured players off the field for treatment, and instructed refs to follow these guidelines or be banished from the tournament. So, there were lots of red cards (15) and yellow cards (227), but it worked. Only three matches, sadly including the Final, ended in 0–0 draws; 141 goals were scored; and the Final was watched by two billion people.

Our beautiful game has had a make-over but have we solved the problem of the drawn game and the need to get a result?

5 – The Golden Goal and the Disappearing Players

No, this chapter is not an episode of Hergé's *Adventures of Tintin*. The title refers to two of the possible alternatives to penalties as a method of resolving a drawn game, as not everyone is a fan of the shoot-out:

Christian Karembeu, French midfielder, following the Euro '96 quarter-final shoot-out against Portugal: 'It is loading a bullet into the chamber of a gun and asking everyone to pull the trigger. Someone will get the bullet, you know that. And it will reduce them to nothing. Fair? Fairness is not even an issue.'

France actually won this shoot-out, which makes Karembeu's comment all the more interesting. His passion is partly explained by the fact that Clarence Seedorf, who missed the crucial penalty for Holland, was his club team-mate and friend. This is what Seedorf had to say: 'I did not volunteer to take the penalty. Nobody does. It is a roulette, but you know that, you have to accept that before you step up to take the penalty.'

Laurent Blanc was the French captain, and scored the winning penalty in the same match: 'Penalties are awful, unfair, but what else is there? The Golden Goal is not the answer. We have seen that in two games already, so clearly it is a waste of time and does not have the right effect.'

Two of Scotland's top managers also looked upon the shoot-out unfavourably. Jock Stein has already been quoted (after Celtic lost a penalty shoot-out against Inter Milan in the European Cup semi-final in 1972: 'We don't consider we lost on football but to a circus turn'). But Alex Smith, Aberdeen's manager after winning the Scottish Cup on penalties against Rangers in 1990, was also unimpressed, despite victory: 'Penalty shoot-outs have nothing to do with football. It's like shooting poor wee ducks at a fairground.'

And Bobby Robson, from his autobiography, on the 1990 World Cup shoot-out between West Germany and England, believed: 'If I had to back one player it would have been Pearce, cool and with the hardest shot in the business. But Illgner saves with his feet and our world caves in. Pearce is distraught. What an unfair burden to put on an individual in a team sport.'

The need to reach decisions without replays is, I think, unarguable, particularly when it comes to the Finals of knock-out tournaments such as the World Cup and the European Championships. Go back to replays and football schedules become unworkable. As a solution to this problem, the penalty shoot-out is felt by the authorities to have worked 'OK'. It has never been considered entirely satisfactory, mainly because it is viewed as providing a 'result by failure' rather than a 'result by success'.

Put another way: everyone remembers Gareth Southgate's miss but how many of us can name all the German players who scored in the Euro '96 shoot-out, or name the keeper who saved Southgate's shot? (Andreas Kopke, in case you were wondering.) Everyone remembers Baggio's miss in the 1994 World Cup Final, but hardly anyone outside Brazil recalls the perfectly executed penalty by Dunga which won the shoot-out and the World Cup.

Dunga scores the fourth penalty for Brazil – World Cup Final, 1994 (Popperfoto)

Fear and Loathing in the United Kingdom

England team managers probably have more reason than most to hate penalty shoot-outs, and Terry Venables eloquently articulates one of the main objections to the shoot-out 'lottery': 'We ought not to be subjecting people to this kind of pressure. Penalties put too much strain on one player. It could ruin his career if he's not a strong character . . . if you feel for the rest of your life everyone could have had a winners' medal but for you, it's a hard thing to get over.'

Simon Barnes, writing for *The Times* during Euro '96, was a little less restrained: 'Penalties are not football. They are not even, as television people are always telling us, great drama. They are cheap melodrama. Melodrama is based on ridiculous exaggeration. Melodrama is bad art as penalties are bad sport

. . . A penalty competition is not to be feared, far from it. It is, in fact, the safest of havens . . . Small wonder, then, that there is a secret, unspoken conspiracy that almost inevitably takes two well-matched teams to the penalty shoot-out. It is nothing less than a conspiracy of fear. There are 120 minutes to play, but in the end, all questions of the blame, all questions of responsibility, can be set aside in the penalty competition . . .

'The Golden Goal. Great idea, wasn't it. All it does is make the fear of catastrophic error still greater, the safety of the penalty competition still more desirable . . . The existence of the penalty shoot-out has become a self-fulfilling prophecy: the last resort has become not so much normal as inevitable. Once we looked forward to the end of the group stages at a leading tournament: the moment when the real football began. Now the knock-out stage is where real football ends.'

The Czech Republic admitted they'd given up on winning a game early on, in order to hold on for penalties. Peter Kouba, their keeper: 'We had a chance because we studied the French penalty takers against Holland.'

The problem of how best to resolve a drawn match is probably the most controversial issue in football today, and has provoked a fierce debate with an amazing diversity of views. The problem is compounded by the fact that no one team, either at international or club level, transcends the modern game in the way, say, Brazil or Real Madrid used to. Basically, there is little between the top sixteen international teams, as was clearly demonstrated in the USA in 1994 and in Euro '96. The same is true of the major European competitions.

In the 1990s only one team has won the European Cup/Champions League more than once: AC Milan in 1990 and 1994. A different team has won the Cup-Winners' Cup in each year of this decade, although Juventus and Internazionale have both won the UEFA Cup twice in the nineties. Nor is the problem going to go away. So, if not the penalty shoot-out, what?

Task Force 2000

Task Force 2000 is an ad hoc consultative committee set up by FIFA after the 1990 World Cup. It was created as a response to the almost universal negative reaction to Italia '90 as a playing spectacle, and to the thousands of proposals for changes in the game received by FIFA after the tournament. As FIFA describes it: 'The Task Force brings together former and current players, club presidents, association officials, coaches, referees, doctors, journalists – a cross-section of the entire football fraternity – to create a fertile breeding-ground for ideas and initiatives for the good of the game.' There is no mention of the fans.

Some of the recent changes in the Laws of the Game originated from the Task Force: the changes to the back-pass law, passive offside and outlawing tackles from behind. As a result, the 1994 World Cup was generally felt to have been a success that redressed the balance. However, these successes were overshadowed by the feeling of anti-climax because the Final was decided by a shoot-out. The Task Force met in Stockholm in June 1995 and decided the best option to the shoot-out was the Golden Goal, although this was not a unanimous decision. At its most recent meeting in November 1996 in Zurich, opinion was again divided. The committee, comprising such eminent figures as Marco Van Basten, Alessandro Del Piero, Platini, Beckenbauer, Cruyff, Roberto Bettega and senior members of FIFA, as well as an impressive array of experts from across the football spectrum, once again demonstrated how difficult a subject this is.

Set out below is a list of the possible alternatives to the shoot-out.

- **The Golden Goal** – sudden death extra-time, where the first team to score wins the match.
- **USA style 'one-on-one' shoot-out** – the penalty taker starts 35

yards from goal and has five seconds to beat the goalkeeper.

- **Corners** – the team awarded the most corners during regulation and extra-time wins.
- **Possession** – the team which has the most possession is awarded the match.
- **Attacking possession** – the team which has the most possession in the opponents' half of the field wins.
- **Disappearing players** – a phased reduction in the number of players on the pitch during extra-time. At regular intervals each team loses a player in an attempt to increase the chances of a deciding goal.
- **A penalty shoot-out before extra-time** – the result of the shoot-out is used to decide the winner in the event the match is still drawn after extra-time.
- **The first goal in extra-time counts double** – in the event there is still a draw after extra-time the team scoring first wins. If no goals are scored then it's back to penalties.
- **The team with the least number of players booked and/or dismissed wins.**
- **Replays** – replay the match until there is a result.

The Golden Goal

The golden goal rule is simple: the first team to score in extra-time wins. It's sudden death. However, penalties follow if neither team scores in extra-time.

The Golden Goal was first experimented with in the World Youth Cup in 1993 and then at the Olympic Games in 1996. It was an attempt to provide that 'result by success' – the scoring of a goal, felt to be absent from the culture of failure surrounding the penalty shoot-out. It was also hoped it would add drama to the period of extra-time.

The early experiments were generally felt to have been a success. However, there was a significant amount of adverse comment when it was first used in a major international tournament in Euro '96. The Golden Goal is, as reported in UEFA's Euro '96 Report, 'unsporting and anticlimactic', and at their post-competition conference in Copenhagen, many national coaches called for its elimination. Nevertheless, it remains FIFA's currently preferred solution and it has some influential supporters, not least of whom is Michel Platini, Co-President of the World Cup Organizing Committee: 'I'm in favour of the Golden Goal. A football match should be decided by an action of play, not some contrived process whose end result is to mark a fine player such as Bossis or Baresi or Baggio for the rest of his career. Of course coaches like the shoot-outs because they can then say that defeat was not their fault. But the people who run the game should take the long-term view. That means keeping the Golden Goal. The philosophy of football is to score goals. If Germany scores a goal in extra-time and wins, that is OK. I think this idea is good.'

Franz Beckenbauer is another fan: 'I played for five years in the USA, and had to get used to the Golden Goal idea over there. But after a short time you learn it and you realize that it can decide a game. I understand all the arguments against it, but it has to be understood that such a new idea simply needs time. It is still too soon to make a final judgement.'

It has some equally impressive opponents, including FIFA President João Havelange: 'The Golden Goal is a sad goal. I prefer penalty kicks before extra-time, so that if the game is still tied at the end it is clear who the winner will be'; Johan Cruyff: 'I don't like the Golden Goal. Time is an important factor in football. If a team scores five minutes into extra-time that should not be the end of the match. I am more in favour of an American-style shoot-out. This is spectacular and not as brutal as penalties, and in my opinion the only real alternative to the Golden Goal or penalties'; David Will, Chairman of FIFA's Referees' Committee: 'It is somehow artificial for a match to end suddenly. It would be better to play out the full length of extra-time, but the first goal during this period could count double.'

The key question is whether the Golden Goal will encourage players to attack. There seems to be little point in introducing such a rule unless you believe teams will accept the invitation to go all out to score the first goal in extra-time.

Sudden death can work in one of two ways. Some players and coaches may see it as a chance to win the game and avoid the risk of losing the shoot-out; others will see chasing the Golden Goal as too risky, and thus play for the draw, hoping to steal a goal on a break-away.

Personally, I doubt whether the Golden Goal will encourage a more attacking approach to extra-time. Many senior coaches agree – Terry Venables, for example: 'The Golden Goal was introduced to make the games more positive and exciting, but I think it has a different effect on teams. They become cautious and more defensive.'

The little evidence to date would appear to support Venables' contention apart, of course, from the semi-final in Euro '96 between Germany and England. It seems England genuinely did try to settle the semi-final in extra-time, and it nearly worked. My sofa still has a mark on it from the glass of red wine I spilt leaping into the air when Anderton hit the post.

I am sure that game, and to a lesser extent the Final, in which the first Golden Goal was scored, had a lot to do with FIFA's decision to persevere with the new rule for France '98. Overall, however, the evidence from Euro '96 was far less positive. Two of the quarter-finals, both of the semi-finals, and the Final itself went to extra-time, and yet only one Golden Goal was scored. More importantly for the spectators, apart from the Golden Goal in the Final, only four goals were scored in those five matches: two in England's semi-final against Germany, and two in the Final itself (one being a Berger penalty). The three other matches were no-scoring draws and went to penalties.

Now, I appreciate these tournaments aren't fantasy football. There is clearly a fine balance to be achieved between the desire to entertain and the need to avoid silly risks. However, if I had been a spectator at, say, the France v Czech Republic semi-final, and had watched ninety minutes of no-scoring football, I would have felt pretty let-down if the game finished with one Golden Goal perhaps only a couple of minutes into extra-time. Indeed, this is exactly how I felt after the Germans' winning goal in the final – a huge sense of anti-climax.

Fans and the players deserve better. Why should the losing team be denied the opportunity to equalize and perhaps win the game? Why deny supporters and television viewers the spectacle of the losing team throwing everything into one final assault, just because it is felt a player might feel upset if he misses a penalty.

Ken Ridden, the FA Director of Refereeing, has some interesting views on the Golden Goal. Understandably he's concerned about aspects of the referee's role.

No one seems to have considered the position of the referee when faced with sudden-death extra-time. The only Golden Goal yet scored in a major international competition illustrates the problem perfectly.

Only four minutes of extra-time had been played in the Euro '96 Final at Wembley when Oliver Bierhoff scored with what was a pretty pathetic shot, woefully mishandled by Peter Kouba, the Czech keeper. Almost before the ball had trickled over the line, virtually the whole of the German bench was on the pitch, embracing the German players and screaming in celebration. However, unnoticed by the referee, Pierluigi Pairetto, linesman Nicoletti had raised his flag, seemingly for an offside against Stefan Kuntz. The linesman dropped his flag after failing to attract the ref's attention, but he had been spotted by the Czech players. They surrounded the referee and persuaded him to consult with Nicoletti. The referee duly consulted the linesman for about thirty seconds, but allowed the goal to stand.

Oliver Bierhoff's Golden Goal that settled the Euro '96 Final at Wembley (Vandystadt)

Now, I have examined this goal very carefully, and it seems to me the referee was perfectly justified in deciding, as I suspect he did, that Kuntz was not interfering with play. However, he would have been a very brave man to have disallowed that goal, particularly with the whole German squad now on the field. The Czech coach, Dusan Uhrin, hinted as much when he said: 'I cannot explain it. We looked up and the linesman had his flag raised, he put it down and raised it again. The referee ignored him. I could not say whether the Germans running on to the pitch to celebrate put pressure on the referee, although it seemed at least a minute until he spoke to his linesman.'

OK, so he would say something like that. But it doesn't negate the principle of this significant objection to the Golden Goal – the unfair pressure it puts on referees if there is the slightest doubt surrounding the validity of the goal. In these litigation-happy days, it does not seem too far outside the bounds of possibility that a major tournament in the future will end up being decided in the courts, the referee's decision to award a Golden Goal challenged on the grounds that no reasonably competent referee could ever have awarded it.

Furthermore, crowd control is a vital part of any big game and an important element of such control is knowing the different times a game may finish. Announcements have to be made, particularly if there is a need to hold one set of supporters in the stadium while rival fans leave. Transport arrangements need to be organized and both these logistical concerns are complicated if you have the possibility of extra-time finishing after one minute. Although the time differences involved are small, an element of certainty is lost.

A Kick in the Grass

The North American Soccer League (NASL) decided that to end a match with a draw was boring and unsatisfying ('as exciting as kissing your sister'). They play a fifteen-minute period of extra-time and then have their shoot-out. They tried the FIFA shoot-out in 1974 but changed to the one-on-one because they thought penalties too 'stereotyped'.

The tie breaking procedure of the NASL involves a penalty shoot-out with a twist. It was recently submitted by the Football Association to the International Board as one of two proposals for an alternative to the penalty shoot-out/Golden Goal:

The rules and conditions of the procedure are as follows:

- The visiting team takes the first kick.
- Each team is entitled to at least five kicks, which are taken alternately.
- If, before five kicks are completed, one team has accumulated an insurmountable number of goals – e.g., one team

scores its first three while the other misses its first three – then the shoot-out is ended by the referee.

- If the number of goals scored by both teams is equal after five attempts, the procedure continues until one team has scored more than the other after both have taken an equal number of kicks.
- Each kicker starts with the ball on the 35-yard-line, and must take his shot within five seconds after the referee's signal is given.
- The kicker and the goalkeeper are not restricted in their movement during the five-second period.
- Only players who are on the field of play at the end of the match may qualify to take kicks.
- No player may take a second kick until all eligible team-mates have had their turn. The order of a team's rotation may vary in each round of kicks.

Initiated in 1977, the American shoot-out was implemented in any NASL game in which a win had not resulted from extra-time, including league games as well as knock-out competitions. All games in the NASL are required to be won or lost – draws have not been allowed since 1975.

While this style of shoot-out has its supporters in mainland Europe and in the UK, it is not favoured by referees. They feel concern for what could happen in a one-on-one moving conflict. What happens if the goalkeeper fouls the penalty taker in close contact? Does the referee send the keeper off, award a penalty, or order the penalty to be retaken?

The Disappearing Team

The second FA suggestion involves the gradual reduction of the number of players on each side at regular intervals as extra-time progresses, the idea being that the greater space available will make it easier to score. Every five minutes or so a player from each side is removed from the field until, presumably, you are left with the two keepers kicking the ball to each other while the referee stands in the middle of the pitch watching the ball pass overhead.

I think we're getting into a slightly weird area here, and it would appear that this was not a really serious proposal. Certainly, the football authorities have a duty to explore any ideas which might make the game more entertaining and fair. However, reducing the number of players at a time when the players are exhausted is not, in my opinion, going to encourage more attacking play. It's also unfair on the players. If the current thinking is to encourage a result based on success, then this idea does not fit the bill. Far more mistakes are likely to occur as exhausted players try to cover more of the pitch as their numbers decrease. Thankfully, FIFA agree. There is absolutely no way this option will ever see a football field.

Corners and Possession

Sergio de Cesare of *La Gazetta dello Sport* in Italy is a contributor to Task Force 2000 and a supporter of using the number of corners won as the way of deciding the winner: 'I am for a collective solution. That means that if a match is drawn after 90 or 120 minutes, the team awarded the greater number of corners should be the winners. This would stop a team from simply defending. Both would be forced to play to win.'

I'm sorry but 'corners' just won't work. If you introduce a rule based on the number of corners won you would have players trying to win corners instead of scoring goals. A player would rather win a corner than go that extra yard to get his cross in. Even worse, players would be instructed to do this by coaches who would feel impelled to cover all eventualities. Electronic scoreboards would show which team was winning on corners as well as goals. Towards the end of a match, teams would know they could win a game by winning, say, a couple of extra corners. You would have the horror of players trying to manoeuvre the ball into the corners rather than score a goal.

According to Ernie Walker, of the Scottish Football Independent Review Commission, this is exactly what happened when corners were used in Scottish League matches during the last war (to make sure that matches were ended on the day). It was a disaster – with twenty minutes to go both teams would stop trying to score goals and try to have corners awarded to them.

David Miller, one of the most respected football journalists in the UK, came up with a possible solution to this problem. Writing in *The Times* after the Euro '96 semi-final shoot-out between England and Germany, he suggested corners as a possible solution, but only corners given away in the goal area. He proposed giving the referee a green card, with which he would signify the award of a 'scoring corner'. The referee would also have discretion as to whether to award such a corner, in order to deal with the possibility of players deliberately playing for a corner.

David Miller's suggestion is a little better, but it puts an impossible burden on the referee. Officials would have to have on-pitch bodyguards if such a law was introduced. And in any event, corners are not necessarily indicative of the way a game has gone. In Newcastle's 1997 European Champions League first-round tie at St James' Park against Barcelona there were 20 corners to 9 in favour of Barcelona, but Newcastle killed them in the first half. If the match had been drawn, why should Newcastle have lost such a game?

Terry Venables rejected the corners idea because he thought it would encourage teams to play a long-ball game in the hope of forcing more corners. His favoured alternative, as explained in *The Best Game in the World*, is to calculate the amount of possession each team has achieved: 'That could be possession all over the field or just in the attacking third. Sky Television have shown the measurements can be carried out instantly, and I'm sure it would help encourage attacking football as well . . . we've got to give every incentive to the team that is prepared to attack . . . So my suggestion is that we play a normal amount of extra-time – no sudden death or Golden Goal – then use the amount of possession each side enjoys as a tie-breaker. If that still doesn't separate the sides, perhaps we could fall back on the number of shots at goal, or on target.'

It's an interesting idea, but one which falls down because it doesn't involve the fans. It's better than corners, but allowing the outcome of, say, the World Cup to be determined by computers in a TV studio is not the answer.

Just as with the corners, the emphasis would be taken away from genuine attempts to attack, and replaced by contrived attacks at the right moment to ensure the computer finds in your favour. Each team would have a new member of their squad (the lap-top computer, possession analyst (sponsored by Microsoft)), who would be calling out possession analysis throughout the match. I suspect it would actually encourage negative play – the nightmare of teams passing the ball around very skilfully without ever looking like they're going to make a serious attempt to score.

There is a general point here. I don't believe anything that occurs as an integral part of playing the game should be used to decide the result of the game in the event of a draw. Deciding a game on the basis of, say, shots on target will simply result in pathetic attempts on goal from way out which stand no chance of beating the keeper.

If we want football to be more exciting, if we want to encourage skilful and attacking play, those issues should be addressed on their own merits. We should deal with the old chestnuts such as abolishing the offside rule, limiting the back-pass rule, just as FIFA have done recently, and reducing the number of foul tackles from behind. We need to support the highly laudable campaign to highlight and promote fair play. Above all, we should be trying to make the first ninety minutes of a game as exciting as possible, not just the thirty minutes of extra-time. We should not seek to merge what are distinct issues.

Penalty Shoot-out before Extra-time

As we have seen, this is the option favoured by FIFA President João Havelange and so warrants serious consideration. Essentially, it involves the current shoot-out law, except the shoot-out itself takes place before extra-time rather than after it. If the match is still drawn after extra-time then the winners of the shoot-out win the match.

The thinking behind this proposal is twofold. Firstly, it is thought that knowing the result of the shoot-out in advance will force the potentially losing team to attack throughout extra-time and thus create more excitement. Secondly, it is felt that having the shoot-out first will reduce the guilt of the player whose shoot-out miss loses his team the match.

While I am loath to criticize any proposal favoured by the FIFA President, there are some flaws in the logic here. If knowing the result in the case of a draw after extra-time is expected to encourage the losing team to attack, surely it is just as likely to encourage the winning team to pack everyone into defence? And the 'guilt' (such as it is) of the player missing in the shoot-out is hardly likely to be assuaged just because the shoot-out takes place first.

The First Goal in Extra-time Counts Double

The full thirty minutes of extra-time are played and the first goal in extra-time counts double in the event of the match still being drawn at the end of the thirty minutes. If there are no goals in extra-time, then a penalty shoot-out would still be used.

Initially, I thought this idea completely barmy. A more obvious invitation for the scoring side to sit back and defend I couldn't imagine. Actually, it's rather subtle. It allows a full period of extra-time to be played and yet encourages teams to attack in the hope of scoring that all-important first goal. If a goal is scored then it forces the losing side to go all out as only two goals will save them from losing. It is akin to away goals counting double, which is a system with which we are all familiar and seemingly happy. I still favour the straight shoot-out, but I think this idea is the next best. My main reservation is the risk of a team scoring once and then shutting up shop, producing a sterile extra-time.

David Will from FIFA supports this idea and, being a FIFA vice-president, his view could carry some weight.

The Team with the Best Disciplinary Record

As far as I can gather, this was not discussed at the last Task Force meeting. However, I have it on good authority that it is an option under consideration and one which deserves slightly more than the cursory consideration afforded to it by most commentators.

Why? Because it fits in nicely with FIFA's ongoing battle to encourage fair play and should encourage attacking football by giving skilful, attacking players more protection.

Replays

Some people think we should go back to replays, but it will never happen. That is not to say that it couldn't be done for the larger tournaments, although it would probably mean teams playing replays the day after the drawn match. The reason replays won't work is much more basic. There is no guarantee whatsoever that the replay will produce a result, and so you are right back to square one, except this time you've added an extra game to the players' burden. What do you do – have a replay and then penalties or the Golden Goal? I don't think so.

Party Bags

As you may have guessed, I'm on the penalty shoot-out team. The real beauty of the shoot-out is not just in its drama, which is considerable and compelling, nor in its brevity or finality (the 38-penalty shoot-out excepted). No, the essential brilliance of the shoot-out is in what I call the 'party-bag' effect.

For those of you unfamiliar with party-bags (lucky you), these are the bags of goodies given these days to all the children who attend a kid's birthday party when it's time to leave. In my day there was no such thing, which meant much more competitive games of pass-the-parcel or musical chairs (you had to win to get a present). Nowadays, children seem much more relaxed about party games, partly because they know that as a result of insane peer pressure the parents of the child giving the party have bought the kids the equivalent of Harrods hampers to take home with them as their 'party-bag'!

An exaggeration, I know, but I tell you, it does become insanely competitive between parents and, sadly, an expectation in the minds of the little guests. 'Can I have my party-bag now?' is a common refrain almost as soon as the party has begun. No doubt derived from some ridiculous research by someone who has never had kids, the party-bag is designed to ensure there are no winners or losers, only winners. Everyone gets a present (the really crazy thing is the birthday boy or girl expects a party-bag as well) and everyone is happy – except the parents funding the party.

The penalty shoot-out is like a kid's party-bag. It does its primary function brilliantly – it provides a dramatic end to a drawn match which involves players and fans alike, obviating the need for replays which no one wants or can afford. But it does more. It allows the losing players and their fans to say to themselves, 'We didn't really lose . . . they couldn't beat us during the game, could they . . . and the shoot-out is a lottery . . . no, we can hold our heads up high . . . we didn't win, but we didn't really lose.' By some voodoo psychology, FIFA came up with a solution which avoids replays, produces compulsive television, and yet lets the losing side feel as if somehow they haven't actually lost.

A Possible Solution

The concluding section of this chapter was originally to have read as follows:

> People say, 'Oh no, not the dreaded penalties . . . it's so unfair . . . the poor guy who misses . . . ruined for life.' Rubbish! Taking a penalty is a skill dating back, as we have seen, to the 1890s – it is as fundamental a part of football as you are going to get. If we have to have a mechanism to decide drawn matches, let's at least have something involving football skills, which is both dramatic and exciting. I think the penalty shoot-out has been a key factor in helping popularize football in recent years, and I suspect, even predict, we will see it become an integral part of even League matches in the next twenty years.

This was written before I had heard from so many people objecting to the penalty shoot-out but not really able to come up with a viable alternative. As I think we have seen, all of the possible alternatives have, admittedly in varying degrees, serious flaws. Ideas designed to encourage more attacking and exciting play end up doing the exact opposite. The fear of losing is greater than the will to win.

I had been a firm fan of the shoot-out, but you can't argue with democracy, and it is clear that a majority of football followers find the shoot-out unfair and unsatisfactory. What can be done?

Perhaps the answer lies in the shoot-out rules themselves. There is a little-known clause, which might provide the answer to the question of how you change the attitudes of players and coaches to losing:

> A penalty shoot-out forms no part of the match itself. It is simply a mechanism to decide which team progresses to the next round or wins a tournament. The match itself is recorded as a draw.

It struck me that this might provide a possible solution to the seemingly insoluble. Matches will not become more exciting unless you change the attitudes of those at the sharp end – the players, coaches, owners and national associations. My suggestion aims to do just that, and involves hitting these people in their two most sensitive areas – their wallets and their pride.

An idea would be for FIFA to be able to say to players and coaches: 'You can play for penalties if you want to, but any tournament actually won after a shoot-out will be deemed a draw. Sure, the Cup will go to the winners of the shoot-out, but each team will receive exactly the same medal – a drawers' medal – there will be no winners' and runners-up medals. Prize money will be reduced if a tournament is won on penalties. There will be no winners' prize money; the two Finalists will share the runners-up money.'

Admittedly, this idea does not work quite so well in relation to earlier knock-out rounds, although the financial sanctions could still apply. Any team winning on shoot-outs will only win half of the prize money it would otherwise have been entitled to – the other half is retained by the organizer or given to the winning Finalist in the event the Final is won without penalties.

I think players might well react to this type of persuasion. No one will want to have a drawers' medal (or will they?) – and so both teams should go all out to avoid the stigma of not really being called the winner. Of course, this could end up being terribly unfair, but maybe the organizing committee could exercise discretion, like the Roman Emperors long ago, to award a 'victory' to a team which has won by way of a shoot-out and which has genuinely sought to win the game in regular and extra-time.

At the end of the day, you can change the rules, reduce the numbers of players, increase the size of the goals, have the players carry on until a goal is scored, but no matter how long it takes, if the players and the coaches don't want to take risks, there is not a lot anyone can do about it. Essentially, the players have to be persuaded, encouraged and motivated into playing attacking football. I'm not saying my idea is the complete answer – I doubt whether there is such a thing. However, I can't help thinking that money is part of the solution. Even Terry Venables admits that, much as he dislikes penalties as a way of deciding matches: 'They can lend a touch of drama to the occasion.'

And, in the words of Gary Lineker, 'He's not wrong.' Twenty-six million people in this country watched the shoot-out against Germany in Euro '96 – one of the largest viewing figures ever.

6 – The Kick

Home Movies

You are 3 years old. Your dad is teaching you to play football in the back garden. You're wearing your brand-new strip – a Christmas present from your uncle. It's a bit big but no one cares. Dad has set up one of the mini-goals and you're taking a penalty. With an exaggerated show of ceremony, Dad marks out a penalty spot and places the ball for you to kick. Mum has the camcorder and Grandma and Grandad are called out to watch as you take a huge run-up. Dad is on his knees playing goalkeeper. You just manage to toe-poke the ball and then fall over. Everyone cheers as Dad (deliberately) dives to the wrong side and the ball trickles into the net. Mum rushes up and gives you a big hug. Grandad starts to wax lyrical about how you're a 'natural', and your dad starts to dream about you playing professionally, just like his dad did when the very same scene was played out thirty-five years before. You love the attention, the feeling of success, and want to do it again and again. The love affair has begun.

Now you're 8 and playing for the local junior league team. It's a crunch game away against your biggest rivals. There are about twenty parents watching. So-called friendly encouragement is, in reality, thinly disguised barracking – parents watching their kids play can be the worst behaved fans of all. Your side are awarded a penalty. There are howls of protest but the handball was blatant and the penalty stands. No one wants to take it so the coach shouts to you. Your dad yells encouragement, so, reluctantly, you pick up the ball and put it on the penalty spot. Suddenly everything goes very quite. No one risks shouting anything to put you off – it will be too obvious who did it, and no one wants to be seen 'sledging' an 8-year-old. You run up, shoot and . . .

You're 16. You're still at school but a Premier League club has you on schoolboy forms. You are the star of the school team. Now when your side get a penalty you grab the ball. There are sometimes a hundred people watching, many of them envious of your skill and success. Some of the supporters are girls, who get excited whenever you go near them on the touchline. It's no longer quiet as you walk back to begin your run-up – the crowd are shouting a mixture of encouragement and abuse. The opposition are whispering, 'Miss it, miss it . . . No bottle, no bottle.' You run forward . . .

Ten years later. You've been playing in the Premiership for over eight years – you made your debut at 18 and never looked back. Last year the club's star striker went to Italy. Now you take the penalties. You've reached the FA Cup Final. It's 2–2 with five minutes to go. You get the ball on the edge of the penalty area, work a brilliant one-two, only the keeper to beat, but you're scythed down from behind. The crowd erupts. The defender is sent off and the referee points to the spot. The physio races on and sprays your bruised calf with some magic potion. Gingerly, you get to your feet and, grimacing, you defiantly motion that you're OK. The fans roar your name. You pick up the ball and place it on the spot. A defender jogs past you to whisper something in the keeper's ear. He's telling the keeper where you're going to put it. You walk back and turn to face the goal. Seventy-two thousand people are screaming their heads off and a hundred photographers are massing behind the net. You run forward . . .

You're 30 now. You are at your peak. You've captained your country through all the qualifying rounds and all the rounds of the finals. Now it's the big one, the dream – the World Cup Final.

Both sides are evenly matched. You try your hardest but, closely man-marked, you cannot break the stalemate. It's sudden-death extra-time. You try for that elusive Golden Goal but the other side has settled for penalties and gets everyone behind the ball. It's a penalty shoot-out.

You take the fifth penalty for your team. As required by the rules you wait in the centre-circle until it is your time to shoot. You watch as each side converts their first three penalties. The other side misses with its fourth but so does your team-mate. You comfort him when he comes back. You don't look as your keeper just fails to keep out their fifth penalty. It's all up to you. There are 100,000 people watching in the stadium, and two billion watching on television. Millions more are listening on the radio. You have to score if your team is not to lose.

You walk forward, slowly and calmly, and put the ball down. As you turn to walk back, the keeper marches forward, complaining to the referee that the ball is not on the spot. It is, but he picks the ball up anyway and replaces it – exactly where it was. The referee yells at him to get on his line. He stands over the ball, remonstrating with the referee, while you walk forward. Then he walks backwards, very slowly, to his line, shouting at you all the way. You re-spot the ball and walk back.

As you turn to begin your run-up, the noise is deafening. The crowd is going wild. For you, though, everything is very quiet – it's all happening in slow motion. You run forward, eyes glued to the ball. With your peripheral vision you notice the keeper jumping around on the goal-line, trying to distract you. You ignore him. You sense, rather than see, the volley of flashlights from thousands of cameras. You ignore them. It seems to take an eternity to reach the ball. Head down, you make a sweet contact and watch . . . as the ball sails over the bar!

'How Could He Miss?'

Not my words, my dad's. And my father was not the first to utter them. I suspect millions of football fans have said exactly the same thing after watching their team miss a penalty.

Most of us, of course, have never had to take a penalty in front of a global audience of two billion people. My father played a reasonable standard of football in his youth, but the biggest crowd he played in front of was measured in the hundreds, not the hundreds of millions. However, he is not alone in his criticism. Francis Lee (arguably the best penalty taker of them all) and Charlie Mitten (17 consecutive penalties without missing) both have fairly trenchant views on penalty-taking, along the lines of, 'If you miss you deserve to be shot.'

Their argument goes as follows: any professional player worth his tax-free bonus should be able to hit whatever target he cares to aim at from a distance of 12 yards – the goalkeeper should be an irrelevance.

Alessandro Del Piero

I watched Alessandro del Piero take two penalties for Italy in Le Tournoi – the four-team competition held in France in the summer of 1997. I was in the middle of writing this book, and had just finished reading some learned papers on the science behind penalty-saving.

My wife, Sue, had already begun to be a little bored with the topic of penalties – I can't wonder why (she's always been intolerant). She was 'watching' the football with me (i.e., she was reading a book in the same room) when Italy were awarded a penalty against Brazil.

'OK, Mr Penalty-kick, you know everything there is to know about penalties. Where's this one going?'

Well, a serious challenge, and one, which I am proud to say, I rose to with aplomb. My research had taught me that Del Piero's run-up had all the hallmarks of the right-footed player aiming for his left – the corner to the right of the keeper, to make it absolutely clear. To this analysis I added the fact he took a pretty long run-up, implying a shot hit with some power. Finally, this was, of course, Del Piero, one of the best players in the world. It seemed logical to assume he was confident of his ability to hit any target he chose. I 'bet the farm'.

As he began his run-up I said, 'He's going to drive it into the top left-hand corner as we look at it. . .'

I appreciate the 'as we look at it' was a little gratuitous, but you have to understand how competitive things can get in the Miller household. Triumphs, no matter how petty, and this one was certainly that, are greatly treasured – particularly, in fact, exclusively, by me. Sue is far more mature. I thought I was remarkably restrained when Del Piero obliged by putting his shot exactly where I'd said he would. Did I jump up, punching my clenched fists skywards and hissing, 'Yes'? Of course I did – earning a thoroughly well-deserved, 'You're pathetic.'

Fast-forward a few days. This time it's Italy v France, and Del Piero has another penalty to equalize. Sadly, Sue has gone out (I can't think why). Same run-up and exactly (and I mean exactly) the same result. You could superimpose the two shots and not 'see the join'. Del Piero was so confident of his dead-ball-kicking ability he didn't care about the keeper. He knew he could hit the ball where the goalkeeper could never save it.

Del Piero's method is the 'classic' one of Lee and Mitten – choose a corner and drive it at three-quarter speed, aiming at the stanchion. Yet, Del Piero, Lee and Mitten all have one thing in common. They have all missed penalties.

Del Piero always puts it to the goalkeeper's right. . .
(Empics)

Great Misses

Before anyone reaches for their notepaper to write a letter of complaint, let me make one thing clear. This is not going to be the chapter where I take cheap shots at all those players who have missed critical penalties. The exact opposite, actually. This is where we try to understand why a professional player, indeed any player, misses penalties, and thus, hopefully, what they can do to maximize their chances of scoring.

As I'm sure most of you know, two of the five players to miss a penalty in a World Cup Final are Roberto Baggio and Franco Baresi, for Italy in the 1994 World Cup shoot-out against Brazil. But can you name the other three? Two were also involved in the 1994 shoot-out: Massaro for Italy and M. Santos for Brazil. The fifth was another Italian, Alberto Cabrini, during normal time in the 1982 Final against West Germany. All five were/are excellent players, but the key individual of these five is Roberto Baggio.

Baggio, I think most people would agree, is one of the finest players ever to have played the game: intelligent, quick, strong, and with two brilliant feet. When you watched Baggio take a free-kick outside the box you felt let-down if he didn't score. His goal against Czechoslovakia in the 1990 World Cup is still up there in many people's lists of all-time great goals.

In the World Cup in 1994 he effectively got Italy to the Final single-handed: two goals against Nigeria, the winner three minutes from time against Spain, and then two brilliant goals in the semi-final against Bulgaria. So, one of the world's great players, possessing exceptional technique and, moreover, a regular penalty taker. One of the goals against Nigeria was a penalty and a more perfect example of the art you are unlikely to see: in off the left-hand post with the keeper diving the other way.

Chris Waddle was very similar to Baggio. I am slightly biased, being a Spurs fan (Arsenal fans should bear with me, I bow down before Liam Brady in a minute), but Waddle is one of the best players I've ever seen, with an incredible ability to hit a dead-ball. Free-kicks, corners – any dead-ball situation – Waddle was brilliant. Ironically, he nearly scored the goal of the decade in the very same semi-final of the World Cup for which he is now famous for all the wrong reasons: a chip from the halfway line which was only just tipped over the bar by Illgner, although the whistle had blown for some infringement I'm still not sure about.

Liam Brady, Graham Rix and Mario Kempes. Brady had the sweetest left foot you could ever wish to see; Rix was a fine player; Kempes was the star of the 1978 World Cup in Argentina and scored two goals in the Final.

Zico, Platini, Socrates, Ryan Giggs, Stuart Pearce, Dan Petrescu, Denis Law, Phil Neal, John Aldridge . . . I could go on and on but you get the point. All these superstars have missed or had penalties saved in critical situations. Why?

Roberto Baggio misses, and the World Cup is Brazil's – USA '94.
(Allsport)

Stress

Pressure is the reason – stress of an incredible magnitude. These guys could hit the inside side-netting with their eyes closed in practice. But let's get one thing straight, right up front. Taking a penalty is not brain surgery. It's not giving birth, landing a plane, confronting an armed robber, changing your first nappy or putting on your first condom. When Bill Shankly said football was not a question of 'life and death – it was more important than that' I don't think he meant it literally. What I think Shankly was trying to say was football has managed to infiltrate the lives of billions of people in a way no other sport has ever done. For millions it has become the 'way of life' for an individual or family. If you took it away you would find a genuine, clinical addiction and millions of people going into 'cold turkey'. Shankly wanted his players to be aware of this – to know what the team's success or failure meant to a great number of people a lot worse off than they were. Winning – scoring that penalty – was not just about win bonuses and huge signing-on fees. It was about making a lot of people happy who, frankly, did not have an awful lot else going for them.

Successfully taking a penalty is not the answer to all the ills of the world. But it does no harm to score one when you have the chance, particularly when all you do is kick a football for a living and, finally, we get to the point: how does a top player ever miss one?

Taking a Penalty

As far as I can see, there are five acknowledged ways of taking a penalty. I would stress that these categories are those within the rules of the game (naked penalty-taking and other perversions are the subject of another book).

The categories for best penalty-taking technique are (in no order whatsoever):

1. Place the ball – either side.
2 Blast – you don't know where the ball is going and hopefully neither does the keeper.
3. Three-quarter-speed drive to the upper corners of the goal.
4. Blast straight down the middle of the goal – a sophisticated version of 2, above.
5. Chip straight down the middle.

There is also, of course, the old 'one-two', as practised by Plymouth Argyle's Jimmy Gauld and Wilf Carter in the 1950s and Ruud Gullit and Jesper Ólsen in the 1980s.

Going back for a moment to the FA Cup Final in 1988. The player who missed was John Aldridge, who was, and probably still is, one of the greatest penalty takers ever. Aldridge was the modern-day master of the 'interrupted run-up' – a style previously championed by Peter Osgood of Chelsea. They were not the first to use this method, however. An unidentified individual, cited in *The Soccer Tribe*, used to run up and deliberately put his foot over the ball without making contact. Then, as the keeper dived, he would calmly tap the ball into the centre of the goal. He claimed it was a way of punishing the keepers for moving before the ball was kicked. Osgood and Aldridge would actually dummy to shoot one side, wait for the keeper to move, and then put the ball the other side.

Not everyone liked it but it was very effective. It is, of course, now outlawed, but only unofficially. There is no law preventing this type of penalty, but referees have been instructed to deem it unsportsmanlike conduct, and order the kick to be taken again.

Prior to the 1988 Final Aldridge had taken eleven penalties that season and not missed one! Then he has to score one in a Wembley Cup Final to equalize Lawrie Sanchez's first-half header. What does he do? He changes his technique, takes a conventional run-up, and Dave Beasant saves it. Admittedly, the save was a good one, but the penalty was not one of Aldridge's best.

Pelé

Pelé always gave the impression that everything he did on the football field was completely instinctive. The control, the vision, the seemingly effortless ability to beat defenders and score with both head and feet; it all just seemed to happen as if pre-ordained. The reality was, of course, hours and hours and hours of practice, starting when he was a small boy, but continuing until he retired.

When he was a boy, he often did not have a proper ball and so, just like many of the great players before and since, he improvised with rags tied together with string, tennis balls, and even a grapefruit. Yes, a grapefruit – Pelé could juggle a grapefruit, using feet, thighs and head, better than most modern players can juggle a ball – if you don't believe me, buy his video.

Pelé was not a regular penalty taker, but he practised taking them none the less, and his training regime for penalties was indicative of the man – the pursuit of perfection. He was not a 'blast-it-anywhere' merchant. To practise he would take four poles – two with red flags on them and two with yellow flags. The red-flagged poles would be stuck in the ground on the goal-line two yards in from each post. The yellow-flagged poles would be placed one yard in from the posts. The aim was to shoot in the one-yard area between the yellow flags and the post – the perfect penalty. As long as the ball didn't go the wrong side of the red flags, Pelé felt confident no keeper would save one of his penalties.

Ironically, for the penalty he took to score his 1000th goal, he drove straight down the middle of the goal, the keeper having moved early and diving to his right. The game was a Silver Cup match between Santos and Vasco de Gama on 19 November 1969. Twelve minutes before the end he was tripped in the penalty area and referee, Manoel Amaro de Lima, awarded a penalty. Rildo came up to take the kick but the crowd started chanting 'Pelé, Pelé,' so the captain gave him the ball. Players from both sides rushed to congratulate him, followed by the reporters, photographers and the crowd. His shirt was torn from his back, replaced with a silver shirt bearing the number 1000, and he was carried shoulder high around the field.

Fireworks exploded and thousands of balloons rose into the sky bearing the message '1000'. Traffic stopped as people danced in the streets. They know how to party in Rio – they just need an excuse. Pelé left the field and came back at the end of the match to unveil a plaque in the wall of the Maracaña stadium commemorating this great achievement. You get the feeling that somehow everyone knew it was going to happen that night, but who cares.

Gary Lineker on Penalties

The penalty kick has always been with us, but it seems to be becoming even more important in the game these days. This is borne out by the fact that several games in the USA '94 World Cup were decided by spot-kicks – either scored or missed! And, in future, it seems highly likely that a great many more drawn Cup-ties will be settled, after extra-time, by the penalty shoot-out.

Whenever a referee awards a penalty, he is dishing out the severest possible punishment to the offending team and giving the offended team a free opportunity to score. It's a simple rule – yet, in the tension of the moment, teams sometimes fail to capitalize on it.

And a fluffed penalty can often mean the difference between winning and losing.

A good striker must be capable of scoring from the penalty spot. It is a skill that should be practised until you are absolutely confident about it. It's certainly no good leaving it to pot-luck when it comes to taking a spot-kick.

And remember, the opposing keeper will have been practising to stop penalty kicks – so you must be as well prepared as he is . . .

Watch the Keeper

Part of the art of the penalty-taking involves knowing the opposing goalkeeper – which way he's likely to dive, whether he tends to move early, and so on.

I realize it's easier to do this in the professional game, where most players are aware of one another's style and are therefore able to prepare in advance – whereas in the amateur game it isn't always possible to watch a keeper before a game. However, even if you don't know anything at all about the goalie, you can get a good idea of what he's like as the game progresses. Is he good in the air? Is he better at diving to the left, or to the right? Is he good at handling hard shots?

Make Your Mind Up

During the week before a match, I would practise my method of beating the opposition's keeper from the spot. And when matchday arrived I would know precisely what I'd do if a penalty was awarded to my team. A good example of this occurred in England's 1990 World Cup quarter-final match against Cameroon.

I had been England's designated penalty taker for almost five years – but in all that time I'd never had a single spot-kick to take! Yet, I was always well prepared and I knew precisely what to do when the ref pointed to the Cameroon penalty spot. I'd been practising for ages to hit it into the corner.

It was a vitally important kick. If I'd missed it we would probably have been on the early flight home. But everything went to plan. The keeper Thomas N'Kono dived really early *and* the wrong way. The ball went in and England lived to fight on.

Then we were awarded a second penalty. This time I was confident that N'Kono would again make an early dive. So, I decided to hit it straight for the middle – and sure enough he obligingly dived out of the way. It proved to be the goal that took us through to the semi-finals.

Another example of forward planning happened in a League match against Norwich. I decided to chip a spot-kick past Bryan Gunn because, again, I knew he was prone to moving fractionally early.

Of course, it could have gone horribly wrong. Bryan might have stood his ground and simply plucked the ball out of the air – in which case I would have looked a proper twit! But I'd done my homework and was confident that I knew his method of dealing with penalties. If I'd attempted to place it in either corner, he might well have saved it.

Remember: once you've decided how you are going to take your penalty kick, stick to that decision. If you change your mind, you'll probably fluff the shot.

Variations

It is important to vary your penalty kicks, and unwise to use the same method over and over again. You can plast them straight, chip them or place them – so the keepers are never sure what you are going to do. When placing a spot-kick, aim for either stanchion at the back of the net.

The Shoot-out

A penalty shoot-out means that 120 minutes of team effort suddenly comes to nothing, and a quick series of one-on-one individual challenges will decide the match. It might be great for the neutral fans in the crowd, and it might make for good television, but believe me, it's nerve-racking for all the players concerned.

A rare miss for Lineker, as Forest's Mark Crossley saves from the spot – 1991 FA Cup Final (Empics)

If your match has to be decided by a shoot-out, don't panic, just take your turn as you would for a normal penalty. If you are the team's regular penalty taker then you'll probably be first in line. Hopefully your shot will succeed and you can then give encouragement to your goalkeeper, and your other team-mates as they take their turn!

Be Quick, Be Calm, Be Confident

Penalty situations are essentially a war of nerves between keeper and kicker. All eyes are on these two players for the duration of the kick. If you are to win the contest – be *quick* and *keep calm*. Don't give the keeper even the slightest hint that you might be worried.

Above all, be confident; make your mind up – and don't change it.

Francis Lee

Francis 'Frannie' Lee, ex-Bolton Wanderers, Manchester City, Derby County and England, and ex-chairman of Manchester City, is a racehorse breeder and trainer, and a millionaire. He is also arguably the greatest penalty taker football has ever seen.

In 1971–72 he scored 15 penalties for Manchester City – 13 in the League and 2 in the domestic Cup competitions. So what, you say, statistics can be used to prove whatever you want, and scoring 15 penalties in one season doesn't mean much if you actually took, say, 30. Fair point. The thing is, in the '71–72 season Lee only took 15 penalties. He didn't miss one.

1971–72 was a unique campaign as far as penalties go. It was the first season played under new, much stricter, guidelines from the FA on the punishment of foul play. Just being awarded 15 penalties in one sason, by today's standards, is quite an extraordinary statistic. In 1972, referees were ordered to crack down on foul play, and, boy, did they obey orders. There was a massive increase in bookings and sendings off, and penalties were awarded at the least sign of anything illegal in the penalty area.

The major beneficiary of the new regime was Lee, by then Manchester City's leading goalscorer and regular penalty taker. City were awarded three penalties in consecutive games at the beginning of the season, all duly dispatched by Lee, who quickly acquired the nickname 'Lee Won Pen', because the first two penalties were awarded for fouls on Lee himself, the popular conception – misconception as it turned out – being that if you so much as breathed on Lee in the penalty area a penalty kick would be awarded against you.

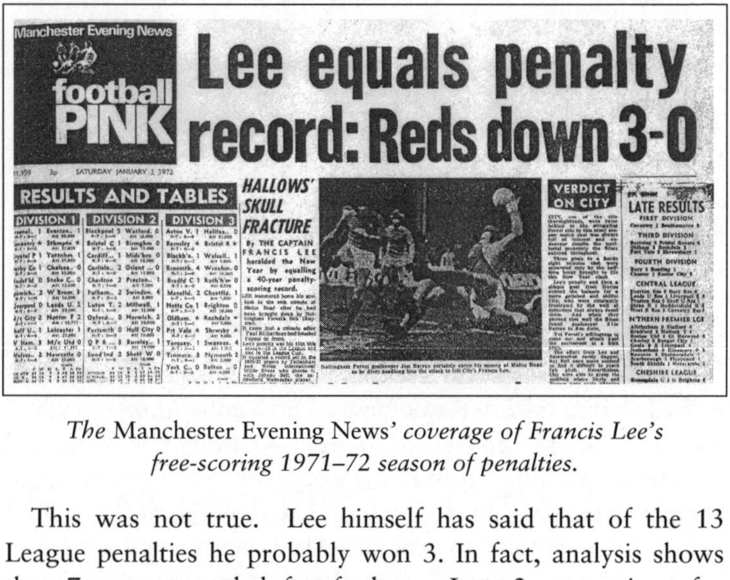

Manchester Evening News

football PINK

Lee equals penalty record: Reds down 3-0

SATURDAY JANUARY 1 1972

RESULTS AND TABLES

DIVISION 1 DIVISION 2 DIVISION 3

HALLOWS' SKULL FRACTURE

By THE CAPTAIN

FRANCIS LEE heralded the New Year by equalling a 40-year penalty-scoring record.

VERDICT ON CITY

LATE RESULTS

FIRST DIVISION

THIRD DIVISION

FOURTH DIVISION

CENTRAL LEAGUE

N'THERN PREMIER LGE

CHESHIRE LEAGUE

The Manchester Evening News' *coverage of Francis Lee's free-scoring 1971–72 season of penalties.*

This was not true. Lee himself has said that of the 13 League penalties he probably won 3. In fact, analysis shows that 7 were awarded for fouls on Lee, 2 were given for handball and the rest for fouls on other City players.

Far from feeling guilty that he perhaps scored more than he should have, Lee believes his record, of which he is justly proud, could have been higher: 'The season I scored thirteen, I should have had a lot more. We had one shot palmed over against Arsenal, and against Ipswich, Mick Mills committed the most blatant handball I have *ever* seen. Neither was given . . . I have always said if I had been awarded the number of penalties I deserved, you could add a hundred goals to my career. I can't think of more than three or four dubious penalties I ever won, and I can tell you umpteen I should have got.'

Penalty Analysis, 1971-72

Competition	Date	Against		Result	Given for
League	18 August	Crystal Palace	h	4-0	Lee fouled
League	21 August	Chelsea	a	2-2	Lee fouled
League	24 August	Wolverhampton W.	a	1-2	Mellor fouled
League	18 September	Nottingham Forest	a	2-2	Unknown
League	9 October	Everton	h	1-0	Young fouled
League	6 November	Manchester United	h	3-3	Lee fouled
League	20 November	West Ham United	a	2-0	Davies fouled
League	4 December	Derby County	a	1-3	Summerbee fouled
League	18 December	Leicester City	h	1-1	Lee fouled
League	1 January	Nottingham Forest	h	2-2	Lee fouled
League	12 February	Sheffield United	a	3-3	Handball
League	4 March	Arsenal	h	2-0	Handball
League	22 April	Derby County	h	2-0	Marsh fouled
F.A. Cup	15 January	Middlesborough	h	1-1	Lee fouled
F.L. Cup	8 September	Wolverhampton W.	h	4-3	Lee fouled

The record in full. Compiled by Manchester City's official statistician, John Maddocks.

This is a story all of its own. In a 1972–73 match against Arsenal at Highbury, Jeff Blockley, the Arsenal centre-half, punched away a Lee shot from under the bar. Gordon Hill, one of the country's top referees, said he failed to see the incident because of the sun in his eyes. The linesman on that side of the field said his view was blocked, so Hill could not give a penalty.

This incident was counterbalanced by another when referee Norman Burtenshaw awarded a goal for City at Spurs when Lee admitted punching the ball in. Like Hill, Burtenshaw didn't see it.

Lee had a column in the Tuesday *Daily Mirror*, and wrote this a few days after:

> No, I'm not suffering pangs of conscience about my grand act of larceny against Spurs at White Hart Lane on Saturday. And before you howl 'cheat', let me explain why I didn't confess to the referee that I'd scored a false winner for City – with my hand.

If I had come clean, I would have been letting down my team-mates and my club. In the grim business of professional football, goals are jewels, and if you have a chance of pinching an illegal one you are bound to do it.

A cynical attitude? Not if, like me, you are convinced that many attackers pot a dozen or more legitimate goals a season that are wrongly disallowed. Not when a single point splits the top four clubs in the First Division Championship, as happened last season.

I feel sorry for the referee, Norman Burtenshaw. My after-match confession exposed him to ridicule, though he had done his job to the best of his ability. But I can say, categorically, if he'd asked me on the pitch about the validity of the goal I would have owned up.

He didn't. He was thirty yards away at the time and I didn't feel justified in running over to him and arguing about his decision. That's the best way of finishing up in the referee's book!

So why embarrass Mr Burtenshaw after the match by admitting hand-ball? The simple explanation is, I was asked a question. And answered truthfully.

These things have happened before and if it happens to me again I will have the cheek to react in precisely the same way.

Lee started taking penalties when he was 17, playing in the Bolton Wanderers reserves. When he graduated to the first team, the manager asked the squad at the beginning of the season who wanted to be the penalty taker. Lee recalls the older players remaining silent, so he volunteered: 'You've got to want to take penalties to be good at it. You've got to enjoy it. The kick itself is the easy part. Any player who can't hit the corner of the goal from 12 yards shouldn't be playing. Nerve is the key.'

Anyone who is really good at something is not short of self-confidence, and Lee was (still is) no exception. On his debut for Bolton, ironically against Manchester City, he scored and was also booked. Later, when he became the acknowledged 'king of the penalty' opposition players regularly used to 'sledge' him as he walked back to begin his run-up 'You'll miss it,' they said (although not in quite such polite language). Lee's response was to wager his week's wages against theirs that he would score. No one took the bet.

Tony Coleman was City's regular penalty taker when Lee joined in 1967, and Lee had to wait until January 1968 before he got a chance to show how well he could do it, after Coleman was substituted against Sheffield United. The following week, in an FA Cup-tie against Reading, City won a penalty; Lee placed the ball on the spot, turned to walk back to begin his run-up, and Coleman nipped in and blazed the ball over the bar! Lee got the job.

At first glance, Lee would appear to be the leading proponent of the 'blast-it' school of penalty-taking. This is another misconception: 'Everyone said I blasted the ball, but I used to aim for the stanchion and hit the ball at three-quarter speed, pretending I was passing the ball 50 or 60 yards. I would take a long run-up to give the keeper longer to think about it; it gave him less of an idea which side I was going to hit it.'

Lee amplified this explanation to me when we met in early 1997. His run-up was always long, and straight (he always lined up directly behind the ball), in order to deny the keeper any clues as to the direction of the shot from his body-language. This was an instinctive approach which has now been vindicated by scientific research (see Chapter 7). Once again, he emphasized the need for decisiveness: 'Pick a corner, turn round, walk back, get totally focused, and then put it in the corner.'

I asked Lee about goalkeepers – was there any one keeper he feared taking a penalty against. His reply may sound cocky, but it was completely free of arrogance: 'I didn't worry about any keeper. I used to stay behind after training and take penalties

Francis Lee, 'arguably the greatest penalty taker of all time'

against the team keepers. I used to take ten penalties when I told them where I was aiming, and ten where they didn't know. I knew if I could beat them when they knew which way the ball was going I didn't have to worry about any goalkeeper.'

Lee is the first to admit he was not infallible from the penalty spot. His penalty-taking experience for England was very unhappy – he took two penalties and missed them both. The first was against Portugal in 1969 where the ground was so heavy his standing foot got caught. 'I was lucky to hit the photographers,' he now recalls. The second penalty was against Wales. He hit it well but the ball struck the underside of the crossbar and cannoned out. He was replaced as penalty taker by Geoff Hurst, whose penalty-taking technique Lee described as follows: 'Geoff just used to blast it, figuring that if he had no idea where the ball was going, the keeper probably didn't know either'.

One of the worst penalties he ever took was, ironically, one which went in and denied Malcolm Allison (later to be Lee's manager at Manchester City) a great FA Cup upset. Lee was playing for Bolton against non-League Bath (then managed by Allison) in a replay on a terrible pitch at Bath. Bolton got a penalty and Lee recalls his then captain, Brian Edwards, saying in a loud whisper as he began his run-up: 'He's due to miss one, you know.' Not terribly helpful. Luckily, the shot went in off the inside of the post, although this was nowhere near where Lee had been aiming. Allison was, apparently, furious, and was to be seen on the touchline jumping up and down on his trademark fur hat.

Two of the most important penalties Lee scored were both in Europe. A penalty for a foul on Neil Young in the European Cup-Winners' Cup Final in 1970 helped Manchester City win a European trophy. The second was for Derby in a European Cup shoot-out in Yugoslavia. Derby won the shoot-out, with Lee taking the fifth penalty and scoring to win the match. The pitch was so wet he deviated from his normal practice and side-footed the ball, sending the keeper the wrong way. Unfortunately, Derby went out in the next round.

Of all the stories Lee tells about his penalty-scoring record, perhaps the best is the tale of his trip to Scandinavia in the summer of 1972. Manchester City were on a pre-season training tour and ended up playing in a tournament against the Swedish national side. City were leading 2–0 when one of their players was injured by a foul for which City were awarded a penalty. While the City player was being attended to, the Swedish keeper approached Lee and said he would like to be the first keeper to save a Francis Lee penalty. Lee thought for a second and then said, 'OK. I'll put it to your right. I won't hit it too hard.' Lee ran up to take the penalty, the Swedish keeper dived to the right, and Lee buried it in the left-hand corner. 'That's how you score fifteen penalties without missing,' he told the disgruntled keeper.

Lee is also the only man, as far as I am aware, to have scored two goals from one penalty kick. He did it in 1972 on the Norwich Six o'clock news programme. He kicked two balls at the same time and beat the keeper with both! I tried to do this in my local park with my 4-year-old son, Jamie, in goal. I nearly broke my ankle.

Bulls – and Outers – from the Penalty Spot

Nat Lofthouse, Bolton Wanderers and England centre-forward (1950–51) from *The Big Book of Football Champions*:

The ball is on the spot twelve yards from goal. All the players, save the fellow who has to take the kick and the opposing goalkeeper are far from the place. It's no distance, there's no hurry, and only the goalkeeper to beat. It's all so simple and straightforward, and with those yards of open space to aim at there's only one place where the ball should come to rest – at the back of the net. On the face of it, that's all there is to it. Yet in their way, penalty kicks are, for me, among the most fascinating of football topics. Weird and wonderful are the ways of the penalty-kick takers, the bulls they shoot, and the outers which are registered from time to time; and no less wonderful are some of the saves brought off by goalkeepers when the penalty shot comes somewhere near them; or the cries which arise from the terraces when a 'sure thing' goes down.

In theory there's nothing to it. In practice there is a lot to it. There are stories of success attached to it – and of tragic failures. It may be remembered that once upon a time Cardiff City failed to become the only club outside England to win the First Division Championship because, in the very last match of the season, one of their players failed to register a 'bull' from the spot. If that has been forgotten then it is not for me to recall the name of the player. The tragedy of such a miss from the point of view of the player!

There are famous players who, having failed to bang the ball to the back of the net from the spot, kept a vow never to have another shot at it. I understand that Joe Smith, the present manager of Blackpool, is among the players under that heading. When he played for the club with which I am now connected, Bolton Wanderers, he was for a long time their regular penalty artist. The day came when he failed, twice in the same match, and that was the end of his record as a taker of these kicks.

It may not have been so easy to score goals from the twelve-yard spot in the days when the goalkeeper could advance to the six-yard line and there do everything he could think of, in the antics line, to put the kicker off. Scoring with these kicks became easier when the goalkeeper's move to the six-yard line was stopped, and even easier still when an additional bar was put up against their movement, when they were ordered to stand still until the taker's foot had actually connected with the ball.

That's the strange part of this penalty business. Right down the line, and even in other respects than those I have mentioned, the law-makers seemed to have one aim in view; that of making the scoring of a goal from the penalty spot more and more child's play. And yet season after season, the stories of failure pile up, in all classes of football. Especially do they pile up in relation to big matches, which means failure by the fellows who are experts. Would anybody care for the job of taking a penalty kick, in the last minute of a Cup Final, with the result of the match depending on whether the ball went home or somewhere else? I wouldn't. Indeed I don't want to take penalty kicks in any match. Danny Howe sees to that so far as the Trotters are concerned.

There is general agreement that Billy Wright is one of the finest all-round footballers in the game in these times. But he himself will tell you that he has no hankering after penalty kicks. Anyway, at Wolverhampton, he is quite happy, because he has Johnny Hancocks to take them, and to score with them.

In passing there's a point there. The possibility of a penalty or penalties being awarded to a side should always be considered prior to the game. And agreement should be reached as to the player of the side who will take such kicks.

On top of that the deputy should also be appointed, because it is always possible that the taker may miss one, and not be at all happy, with his confidence shaken about taking another which may come along.

Another strange thing occurs to me. The experts in the penalty-taking line, of our time, occupy different positions on the field, although an old-time fashion for goalkeepers to take the penalties at the other end of the field seems to have gone out. I have mentioned a couple of wingers who make a good job of it. Two of the full-backs connected with nearby London clubs are the penalty takers for their teams: Wally Barnes for Arsenal and Alf Ramsey for Tottenham Hotspur.

Just as players in different positions take them, so there are widely differing views as to the straightest road to success. Wally Barnes, for instance, believes that the best way is to give the ball everything he has got. By this method Barnes registers bulls too. The argument in favour of this method is that if, by chance, the ball is not hit so wide of the goalkeeper that he can't get a hand to it, the force behind the ball may still carry it onwards.

Alf Ramsey, for his part, puts his faith in a well-placed shot which doesn't so much depend on force as it depends on the ball going inside at the place to which the goalkeeper can't very well get. In respect of this type of shot, the quite reasonable argument is that nature has made it much easier for any of us to throw out our arms than our legs. But a shot meant to go just inside the post doesn't leave much margin for an error of any kind.

Peter Doherty has scored many goals from the spot by changing his shooting foot at the last moment. Shaping as if to hit the ball with his right foot, he would really hit it with his left. That's one of the things the penalty taker has to try to do, deceive the goalkeeper as to where he means to put it.

Again, the story of goalkeepers is worthwhile. Some are able to swing to the right or to the left much quicker than the other way round. But when one notes the agility of such goalkeepers as Bert Williams, Sam Bartram of Charlton, Jim Sanders of West Bromwich Albion, and so on, the impressions convey that they have no 'blind' side, that they can move either way with equal smartness.

And there we come to another of the reasons why goals aren't scored from the spot. True, there's only the goalkeeper to beat. But *only* is a big word.

7 – The Save

A Keeper's Nightmare

You are a goalkeeper. You are asleep and you're having a nightmare. It's the Final of the European Champions Cup at Wembley. The game is tied, notwithstanding a Golden Goal period of extra-time, and now it's a penalty shoot-out. Up to this point, you've not actually played any part in the game. You came on as a substitute for the first-choice keeper in the last minute of extra-time. You've not played for one simple reason: you're not really very good at goalkeeping. You can't catch corners or crosses to save your life. Your positional sense is non-existent and you are useless at kicking the ball when it is passed back. However, you can save penalties. You are a wizard with a lap-top computer and brilliant at assessing body language. You are the team's specialist penalty stopper – saving penalties in penalty shoot-outs is all you do.

While the referee is organizing the shoot-out, you secretly examine your laptop's data on the opposing penalty takers. This is where your nightmare really begins, because the opposition eleven on the pitch at the end of extra-time are (in no particular order):

1. Luis Chilavert – the Paraguayan international goalkeeper. Not only is he a free-kick expert; he likes taking penalties. He once scored a free-kick from near the halfway line in a match between his club, Velez Sarsfield, and River Plate of Argentina. In a World Cup qualifying game in 1996 he scored a penalty for Paraguay against Argentina in front of a capacity crowd at the River Plate Stadium. The week before he had said: 'I hope that God will give me a chance to take a penalty and to score a goal.'

   So, a kick like a mule and a hot-line to the Big Man upstairs.

2. Roberto Carlos – Brazilian wing-back, and one of the stars of the current Real Madrid side. Allegedly able to make the ball talk and go round corners, he has a harder kick than Chilavert.

3. Julian Dicks – West Ham and England full-back. Dicks epitomizes the word 'hard'. I love watching Dicks take a penalty: he takes a huge run-up, his eyes never leave the ball, and he has a kick with his left foot that could launch a satellite.

4. Ari Haan – Dutch midfield star of the 1970s. He hits the ball so hard he probably thinks taking a shot from 12 yards is too much like cheating. In the 1978 World Cup, he scored a goal from 35 yards out against Sepp Maier (the keeper didn't even move).

5. Peter Lorimer – Scotland and Leeds winger. Specializes in rocket-like volleys and free-kicks which scream into the roof of the net. During the 1970s he was felt to have the hardest shot in British football. A recognized penalty taker.

6. Charlie Mitten – 'The Bogota Bandit', so-called because he was one of the first UK players to go and seek the big money in South America. He scored seventeen consecutive penalties in the 1950s.

Eusebio smacks one past Gordon Banks – World Cup semi-final, Wembley, 1966 (Hulton Getty)

7. Geoff Hurst – star of the 1966 World Cup. Francis Lee described Hurst's penalty-taking technique as: 'He just blasted it, he felt that if he didn't know where it was going, the keeper sure as hell wouldn't.'

8. Francis Lee – arguably the best penalty taker of them all.

9. Rivelino – Brazilian wing wizard. He scored a goal in the 1970 World Cup with one of the hardest shots I have ever seen (until Roberto Carlos came along). Playing for his club, Corinthians, he once scored straight from the kick-off. The Rio Preto keeper, Isadore Irandir, had a habit of praying in his goalmouth at the start of each match. As the Corinthians kicked off, Irandir took up his praying position, only to hear Rivelino's shot from the centre spot whistle past him into the net.

10. Eusebio – Portuguese and Benfica star of the 1960s. Nice guy. Thunderous shot. Likes smashing the ball at goal-keepers from short range – ask Alex Stepney of Manchester United.

11. Roy of the Rovers – the player every coach would like to have on his team. Noble, gifted, courageous; scriptwriters never let him miss a penalty. At the last count he had scored 50.

Your side lose the toss and you have to face the first penalty. The opposition's first five penalty takers are, in order: Carlos, Lee, Hurst, Eusebio and Rivelino.

Just as your penalty coach has taught you, you go through your 'shoot-out' routine. The computer analysis has been examined, now you must factor in the penalty taker's body-language. First the run-up.

Carlos places the ball on the spot and, turning his back on you, walks away from the ball. He keeps on walking . . . and walking. He walks back so far he could be a West Indian fast bowler. Your computer seems to have got it right – it appears Carlos is going to blast it.

Unstoppable Penalties

Any supporter of Real Madrid, or anyone who saw Le Tournoi in the summer of 1997, could have told you as much. In Le Tournoi, Carlos scored the most extraordinary free-kick most people have ever seen. Roughly 35 yards out, and in the centre of the pitch, he bent the ball around the French wall with the outside of his left foot, imparting such a vicious swerve on the ball the ball-boy six yards to the right of the goal ducked, thinking he was going to be hit. Instead, the swerve brought the ball back as though it was radio-controlled, and it went in off the inside of the right-hand post. While this particular free-kick wasn't timed, Carlos has taken free-kicks in the Spanish League timed at approximately 85 miles per hour!

Thankfully for goalkeepers everywhere, Roberto Carlos is not the regular penalty taker for Real Madrid. Unfortunately for your dream, he is the first up in the shoot-out. As he turns to begin his run-up thousands of supporters make the sign of the cross. They are praying for you. What are your options?

You could stand to one side of the goal and let him shoot into an empty net, thus avoiding the possibility of death or serious injury. However, this would probably not prove very popular with your manager, fellow players and fans. So, the options would seem to be as follows:

- Stand your ground in the middle of the goal and hope that Carlos either blazes the ball over the bar or wide of the posts.
- Stand your ground and, while recognizing you may have to go to hospital, hope he drives the ball straight at you and your body deflects it.
- Pick a side and dive, hoping either that you get it wrong – but at least you tried – or that the ball hits you in mid-air and doesn't go in. This will give you the consolation, as you sit in your hospital bed, of knowing you saved a Roberto Carlos penalty.

Roberto Carlos and all the other players in your nightmare are the perfect exponents of what we already know: it is almost impossible to save a well-struck penalty. You can analyse data until your hard disk disintegrates; you can be the greatest body-language expert in the world, hone your reaction times until you could beat Ben Johnson (on steroids) out of the blocks – some penalties, though, are quite simply unstoppable.

All this is true, but the situation is not as gloomy as it may seem. You may be wondering about the references to computers and body-language in your 'nightmare'. Well, with the help of science (and a great deal of practice) goalkeepers can improve their chances of saving a penalty.

'Hold on,' I hear someone cry from the back. 'Who are you to instruct us in the art of penalty-saving? What are your goalkeeping credentials? Why should we listen to what you have to say?' No reason whatsoever, actually. I am not, nor have I ever been, a goalkeeper. On the few occasions I have kept goal I have been universally acclaimed as one of the worst players ever to stand between a set of goalposts. Unkind references to my Scottish ancestry would fill the air. Please do not stop reading. My contribution relates to improving your sex appeal, and can be found at the end of the chapter. First, saving penalties, and the keeper's great dilemma.

To Move or Not to Move . . .?

As we have seen, the early years of the penalty were characterized by keepers moving before the ball was kicked and saving most kicks. The real advantage in moving early lay in the ability to move forward. As most keepers will tell you, one of the critical factors in saving any shot is 'narrowing down the angle'. Put more simply, you need to give the striker less of the goal to aim at. The closer you get to him the less of the goal he can see. In the case of Willie Foulke, the striker sometimes couldn't see the goal at all!

As soon as keepers were forced to stand on the goal-line and not move their feet everything changed: the save became a rarity. Then, in July 1997, FIFA turned back the clock. Together with a number of other law changes, the penalty law was amended, and keepers once again can move, albeit only sideways along the goal-line, before the ball is kicked . . . should they so wish.

The reason for the change was a combination of pragmatism and guilt. For years, virtually every keeper in the world has moved before the ball is kicked, with hardly any referees enforcing the law requiring them to stand still. After Italia '90,

Ken Ridden, FIFA's Head of Refereeing, did an analysis of all the penalties taken in that tournament. He kindly lent me the video he prepared from this research as a teaching aid for referees. It shows not one penalty taken in conformity with the laws of the game as they then stood, and yet not one was retaken. The same was true of Euro '96.

Through lack of observance, the law had effectively changed itself, and the authorities felt there was no real downside in formally recognizing this. FIFA were also feeling guilty because of the increasing pressure placed on keepers over the last few years to speed up play. The back-pass rule was tough enough, but when they prohibited keepers from picking up throw-ins, the authorities clearly had a pang of conscience. There was the feeling that they had perhaps been a little too beastly to keepers. So they threw them a concession: they came up with the idea of legalizing something keepers did anyway.

FIFA does not believe the new law makes penalties easier to save, primarily because referees have been told to get tough on any forward movement. Referees have also been encouraged to order retakes should there be any other infringements when a penalty is being taken. Prior to 1997, infringements at penalty kicks, or persistent moving by the keeper, meant a caution. This tempted referees to allow goals to stand, even though an offence had been committed, because they were reluctant to book players for such minor offences.

Now, offences such as encroaching into the box no longer result in an automatic booking, although repeated encroachment or persistent forward movement by a keeper after being warned, could result in cautions for ungentlemanly conduct. So, expect to see a lot more penalties being retaken.

As the new law took effect in August 1997, Peter Schmeichel spotted the potential for distracting the taker in the pre-season friendly against Inter Milan when Manchester United lost on penalties. 'Their keeper did it so well he succeeded in putting off Jordi Cruyff and Nicky Butt,' he claimed. In the *Sunday*

Times George Graham, Leeds' manager, believed the new law was designed to let refs off the hook: 'Allowing a goalkeeper to dance about on the line is a way out of the constant criticism that he moved when a penalty was being taken. With the eagle-eye of television, the referee was often shown to be wrong, so now he has a get-out. But there will still be replays whenever the keeper moves forward off the line, which is still not allowed, so it will solve nothing. Far worse to me is the thinking, if any, behind it at all, because the side that has committed the offence is going to have a better chance of escaping punishment and we will see more penalties saved this season than ever before. I've spoken to Nigel Martyn about it, told him my views, and he shares my concern.'

Kevin Pressman, the Sheffield Wednesday keeper, was trying to perfect a technique that would allow him to take the best advantage of the new regulations: 'I can see all sorts of things coming in, anything to unsettle the penalty taker. If it works and you get them to blast it over the top or you save it, it's one up to the keeper.'

Peter Schmeichel saved two penalties in the penalty shoot-out to decide the Charity Shield on 3 August 1997. With the first, taken by Frank Sinclair, Schmeichel clearly moved and made Sinclair change the direction of his shot at the last second. 'Moving on the line is going to cause a lot of confusion during the first couple of months of the season both for keepers and shooters. You have to try these things to see where the advantage lies,' said Schmeichel.

Bob Wilson, meanwhile, claimed, 'I've talked through the implications of the penalty-rule change with David Seaman and we believe the length of the taker's run-up is crucial. Hopping about on the line will put the taker off if he uses a long run-up, but if the taker uses only one step the keeper is asking for trouble. However, David has such a good record for saving penalties, he is unlikely to change a system that works.'

Trivia alert: in 1945 Tommy White, Kilmarnock's left-half,

David Seaman: 'a good record for saving penalties' (Sportsphoto)

took a penalty seven times against Partick Thistle. On each of the first six shots the referee ruled the keeper had moved and ordered a retake. The seventh penalty was taken to the referee's satisfaction, and the keeper saved it!

So, keepers can move again. But moving before the ball is kicked is only of benefit if it increases the chance of making a save, and a lot will turn on how strict referees are in forbidding forward movement. We will see by the end of this chapter that a strategy based on moving early is probably the wrong one, but before you decide whether to move or not, the first thing you have to do is simple: guess correctly where the ball is going to go.

'Guessing' doesn't sound terribly scientific, but it does once termed 'anticipation'. What's more, we now know that you can improve your anticipatory skills using a combination of sensible observation, analysis, evidence of past experience, and lots of practice. The first ingredient you need is information. Facing a penalty is a classic 'one-on-one' confrontation, and, as Gary Lineker says, the first thing you need for any conflict is to know as much as you can about your opponent.

Know Thine Enemy

It is rumoured Pat Jennings, the great Spurs, Arsenal and Northern Ireland keeper in the 1960s and 1970s, kept a dossier on all First Division penalty takers. He collected information on each penalty taker's technique, and made careful notes after each penalty he faced. This gave him an edge when it came to guessing which way the ball was going and how hard it would be struck. (Of course, Gary Lineker did the same sort of thing when it came to goalkeepers.)

So, first of all, find your information. Data on international, Premier League and indeed, virtually all professional players, is relatively easy to obtain – almost every penalty taken these days is televised or reported. It's more difficult if you play in a Sunday League on Hackney Marshes. Given the lack of published information on amateur penalty takers, keepers are forced to rely on more anecdotal sources of information. But beware. The title of this book is derived from an example of just such a piece of anecdotal evidence which went horribly wrong.

I was 16 and playing for a team organized by a school-friend against his big brother's Sunday League side in a pre-season warm-up match. Anthony's brother's side were awarded a penalty in the first half (a scandalous decision, as I recall), at which point Anto (classic football nickname) went into his helpful captain routine. He went to our keeper and told him that his brother, who was taking the penalty, 'always puts it to the right'. This advice was passed to our hapless goalkeeper during a whispered meeting on the goal-line, with Anto's brother waiting impatiently to take the kick. Anto gave me a big wink as he trotted back.

As you will have already worked out, Anto had failed to make clear to our keeper whether his brother always put the ball to his right or to the keeper's right. You can guess the rest. A confident and dramatic dive by our keeper to his right while the ball trundled gently into the other corner. We lost 1–0.

The 'Jennings' approach was nothing new. Ted Sagar, the famous England and Everton keeper, was working along the same lines just after the Second World War. This is what he had to say in a 1950 article on goalkeeping entitled 'The Proper Use of Head, Hands and Feet':

> It [the head] has to do a lot of thinking for there is always something for the goalkeeper to learn. What sort of shot is most likely to come the way of the goalkeeper from a particular angle, for instance. Try playing as a scorer, rather than as a goalkeeper, by way of a change, and find the probable answer to that one. There are players, even penalty takers, who have a pet way of shooting. Think about them. Of course we goalkeepers think. It's life-time study . . . One of the things which have been said about all the best goalkeepers is that they made the job seem really easy. In other words, they had the art of anticipation highly developed.

Ron Springett played as first-choice keeper for England and played in the World Cup Finals in Chile in 1962. He said this in 1965:

> When facing a penalty, the tables are turned (compared to a corner) and you are at a great disadvantage. There is only one thing to do – take a gamble and fling yourself one way in the hope that the penalty taker has chosen the same side as you have done. By standing still your only chance of saving comes if the marksman hits the ball straight at you, or miskicks: and how seldom that happens nowadays!
>
> I've made mental notes about all the penalty takers I've seen in action. There are some who have a definite preference for shooting to one side, invariably their better one. If that is the case, in facing up to the marksman I stand a little off-centre on his favourite side, hoping to encourage him to change his mind and shoot on his weaker side.
>
> I realize that I'm taking a long shot, but if it means saving one penalty in a hundred it is well worth taking.

So, Sagar thought about it, Springett made mental notes, and Jennings wrote notes in a book. The approach is considerably more high-tech these days, but the basic thrust remains the same. The most effective exponents of this data-based approach are, predictably enough, the Germans. Past-masters of the penalty shoot-out, the Germans have brought penalty-saving into the computer age.

Notebooks to Lap-tops

In the 1997 UEFA Cup Final, Schalke 04 were playing Inter Milan. The second leg was played at the San Siro and went to penalties. Advantage Inter, you would have thought – a penalty shoot-out in the San Siro? They had to be favourites.

However, what Inter didn't know was that Schalke had a secret weapon.

Schalke's coach, Huub Stevens, had fed all the data he could find on Inter's players' past penalty-taking techniques into a computer (rather helpfully, Inter had lost the semi-final of the Italian Cup to Napoli on penalties just a few weeks previously). The results gave Schalke's keeper, Jens Lehman, a good idea where each opponent was likely to place the ball. No guarantee, but certainly something to work on. Schalke duly won the shoot-out 4–1.

The all-important first kick for Inter, taken by Zamorano, was saved. Then both Aaron Winter and the next kicker missed. Ironically, the French star, Djorkaeff, was the only Inter player to score (he'd missed out on a Euro '96 Final when losing to the Czech Republic on penalties in the semi-final).

Jens Lehman later explained his secret weapon: 'I had checked the lap-top and whenever Zamorano took a long run he always kicked it to the left. And that's exactly what he did.'

One sort of feels this must have been illegal, but I can't think of any law Lehman infringed, unless you consider what he did ungentlemanly conduct – which is surely a little harsh.

It makes you think, doesn't it? The Germans have not lost an international penalty shoot-out since 1976. They have missed only one penalty – yes, one – in all that time. Uli Stielike missed his penalty in the shoot-out against France in 1982.

In the Euro '96 shoot-out against England, Andreas Köpke guessed correctly on the direction of every England penalty, apart from the first one by Shearer. Gareth Southgate's penalty was the only one he saved because all the other penalties were so well struck. It may just be a coincidence, but the only other penalty Southgate had taken before that fateful evening was for Crystal Palace in the last minute of their vital Premier League relegation battle against Ipswich in 1992–93 (he had never taken a penalty at Premier League level before). He hit the post, the match was drawn 2–2, Palace were relegated on goal difference, and Ipswich stayed up. Southgate remembered this penalty when interviewed before the Germany match: 'I've only taken one penalty before, for Crystal Palace at Ipswich. It was 2–2 in the 89th minute, I hit the post and we went down that year. But I think I'd be far more comfortable now than I was then.'

The post Southgate hit was the left post as he looked at the goal. The penalty in Euro '96 went to the same side as the Crystal Palace penalty, at the same height and at the same speed. (Cue *X-Files* music.) A German striker said after the game that they hadn't been practising penalties, but what about the keeper? Is it too far-fetched to think they had checked out all the previous penalties taken by the English players – somehow I don't think so. The truth is out there.

At this point, I sense a whole lot of you standing up like schoolchildren with their hands raised saying, 'Ah, but what if the penalty taker pulls a fast one? What if he changes from his favourite side? What if he goes for the double-bluff? What if he's put it to his left for his previous five penalties and guesses you're going to guess he's going to change and put it to his right? So he puts it exactly where your research told you he would . . . and you dive the other way. Where's your research now, smarty pants?'

A perfectly reasonable point. Just because a player has side-footed the ball to the right of the keeper in three previous matches, does not mean he will take every penalty that way. Historical precedent should never be the sole factor determining future approach. It is merely one part of an information jigsaw which, joined with various other pieces, can help a keeper make the right decision. However, combine it with the use of 'Advance Cue Utilization' and you are 'smoking'.

'Here Comes the Science Bit . . . Concentrate'

Ok, so I'm not as sexy as Jennifer Aniston from *Friends* when she does her shampoo advert. However, this is the 'science' part, and I think (hope) it will be worth concentrating. Now for the bad news. The science part requires you to understand some physics! I know, I know, the very word brings me out in a cold sweat too: visions of incomprehensible electric circuit diagrams, 'slinkies' illustrating wave theory, and eccentric teachers. Don't worry. The physics part really only involves appreciating how fast a football travels, and how quickly a keeper has to react in order to make a save.

It came as a big surprise to me how little scientific research has been carried out on penalty-saving. As I surfed the Internet (desperately trying to resist the lingerie web-sites) I felt sure there would be a vast reservoir of material, particularly post-Italia '90. In fact, the two key pieces of research are dated 1989 and 1997 – I've not found anything meaningful in between. Moreover, hardly any of this research has filtered through to the general football playing/watching public. This is doubly surprising because it is clear goalkeepers need all the help they can get. In this case I believe the statistics do not lie: keepers, even the very best, are not good at saving penalties.

Two Canadian scientists at the University of British Columbia in Vancouver, Dr Ian Franks and Tod Harvey, recently reviewed all of the 138 penalties taken in World Cup finals between 1982 and 1994. Their research shows that even the most expert of keepers are unsuccessful when it comes to predicting the direction of a penalty kick, let alone saving one.

Of the 138 penalty kicks analysed, 77.5 per cent resulted in goals, 8 per cent of shots missed the target, and 14.5 per cent were saved by the keeper. More importantly, keepers correctly predicted the shot direction in only 41 per cent of shots. Clearly, keepers need help.

Reaction Time, Anticipation and Body Language

Three pieces of research carried out in the late 1980s appear to be the first real scientific attempts to understand what is going on at a penalty kick in football. Amazingly, more research had been carried out into anticipation for cricket batsmen and ice-hockey goaltenders than for football goalkeepers. However, W. Kuhn in 1988 produced a paper entitled *Penalty Kick Strategies for Shooters and Goalkeepers*.

In this paper, Kuhn described a kick faster than 75km per hour as fast, and anything below this as slow to medium-paced. Kuhn showed that a medium-paced shot (20.83 millimetres per second) takes 600 milliseconds to reach the goal. A very fast shot – 27.77 millimetres per second – takes 400 milliseconds to reach the goal. For a keeper to save a penalty struck at more than 20.83 millimetres per second Kuhn showed that he must initiate his movement before or at the point of foot–ball contact.

Franks and Harvey at the University of British Columbia in Vancouver seem to confirm Kuhn's findings on the time it takes for a kick to reach the goal. Their analysis of all the penalty kicks from the last four World Cups showed that the average time from ball contact to the ball crossing the line was 600 milliseconds. The movement time for goalkeepers – the time from first movement to the time any part of the keeper's body crossed the possible path of the ball – ranged between 500 to 700 milliseconds. As these times are approximately equivalent, it follows that keepers need to begin their response as the ball is being contacted at the very latest. Factoring-in reaction time of between 80 to 144 milliseconds effectively means the keeper needs to move approximately 100 milliseconds before foot–ball contact. Only if the ball is struck at a speed considered 'soft' can the goalkeeper wait until after the ball is kicked to make his move. As the keeper can never know for sure what the ball velocity will be, it is important he begins his movement, at the latest, at foot–ball contact. He therefore needs to use some form of perceptual anticipation in order to determine the direction of the flight of the ball.

In non-scientific language, this means he needs to make an 'informed guess', based on whatever information is available to him. Assume for the moment he has consulted his lap-top computer and the data shows a preference for a side-footed shot to the penalty taker's right. Which is all fine and dandy, but the player has been known to put it to the other side, and has even blasted it straight down the middle on one occasion. More information is required on his immediate intention. This can be provided by the penalty taker's body language as he runs up to and kicks the ball.

In the late 1980s, research was carried out on something called Advance Cue Utilization by Dr Mark Williams, now of John Moore University in Liverpool. This followed research by a group led by T. McMorris of the West Sussex Institute of Higher Education, which had begun to identify the types of pre-impact cues used by goalkeepers in anticipating ball direction. McMorris's study also noted the significant difference between guessing the direction of the kick and guessing the height. During interviews after the experiment, the keepers identified the point of foot–ball contact, angle of the player's trunk and angle of run-up as the main pre-contact and contact cues.

Dr Williams took the research a few steps further. Now it's time to really concentrate – the exact methodology of Dr Williams' research may seem a little complicated but it is important. It has some significant consequences for training methods.

The objective of the research was to examine the effect of playing experience on anticipatory performance during a penalty kick. The investigation also sought to identify any specific input cues which allow players to anticipate ball direction.

A filmed occlusion paradigm was used where the perceptual display available to a goalkeeper during a penalty kick was selectively manipulated by varying the duration of the kick that was visible. (Translation: A video film was used, with the film being stopped at various key moments during the taking of a penalty kick.)

The test film included 40 penalty kicks taken by right-footed players. The camera was placed in the goalkeeper's normal penalty position and each filmed trial included the penalty taker's preparatory stance, run-up and kicking technique up to the point of occlusion. Four restricted viewing conditions were used: 120ms before foot–ball impact, 40ms before impact, at impact, and 40ms after impact.

Two groups – 30 experienced goalkeepers and 30 inexperienced keepers – viewed the penalty kicks on a video projection screen. The experienced group had each played an average of 396 competitive football matches, the inexperienced group an average of 56 each. They were all required to make judgements regarding which corner of the goal the ball was directed to on each penalty kick at the various stages of the film. They also completed a questionnaire following the session, from which was obtained information regarding the importance of various areas of the penalty taker's technique in anticipating ball direction.

An analysis of the responses showed significant differences in performance between the groups and across the different times at which the film was stopped. The main conclusions to be drawn from the experiment were as follows:

- Experience plays a major role in the ability of goalkeepers to make use of advance visual cues in anticipating ball direction.
- Differences between experienced and inexperienced players were more apparent at earlier occlusion periods, with experienced players being able to make better use of earlier potential sources of information.

- The superior performance of the experienced players was significant only under the shortest durations – pre-impact conditions 1 and 2.

More sophisticated statistical analysis showed that both groups scored significantly better than 'chance' across all conditions. 'Chance' for the purposes of the experiment was set at 25 per cent. (You could guess to go left or right, high or low – i.e., to one of four corners – a one in four chance of getting it right just by guessing.) The results of the experiment proved you could do a lot better by anticipating the direction of a penalty kick from the preparatory movements of the penalty taker.

The questionnaire responses thus took on an added importance. If it was possible to anticipate the direction of the ball, what visual cues should you be looking for? The responses revealed that information was obtained from:

- Angle of run-up.
- Arc of leg on approach to the ball.
- Angle of kicking foot prior to ball contact.
- Angle of hip prior to ball contact.
- Angle of trunk on ball impact.

The most important of these information sources was found to be the hip position just prior to the point of impact. If the right hip was in an 'open' or angled position relative to the goalkeeper, the ball went to the kicker's right. If the hip was 'square on' to the subject, the ball went to the kicker's left.

Similarly, the lean of the trunk was deemed to be the most important factor in anticipating the correct height of the ball. A ball that went high was characterized by a leaning back of the trunk on ball impact. If the trunk tended to lean forward, with the head and shoulders over the ball, then the kick kept low.

In Dr Williams' experiment, further analysis revealed the majority of errors (61.8 per cent) were associated with incorrect height judgements. In contrast, very powerful differential cues seemed to be available in distinguishing the correct side, where only 25.71 per cent of errors occurred. Error rates for incorrect height decisions showed that there was a marked improvement in height judgement only after initial ball trajectory had been viewed. In contrast, the error rate for incorrect side was relatively low even under the earliest occlusion period.

Based on these findings, the author came up with some suggestions for a penalty-saving strategy:

- Goalkeepers should attempt to anticipate the direction of a penalty kick prior to foot–ball contact.
- Information regarding the correct side should be extracted from the run-up, kicking leg and, specifically, the hip position prior to impact.
- Adjustment of position according to shot height should occur initially on the basis of trunk position prior to foot–ball impact, but firstly on the basis of the initial portion of ball flight just prior to breaking ground contact in the diving phase.

We will try to make some sense of all this in a moment. What is almost more interesting is the second experiment Dr Williams carried out following the success of the first. The objective was to determine whether a beginner's anticipatory performance could be improved by a video-based coaching programme.

Ten novice players were selected from the first experiment to participate in approximately ninety minutes of visual simulation training using video film. Relevant anticipatory cues, drawn from the questionnaire study administered in experiment 1, were highlighted using the video film of six different penalty takers. The training film included a total of 48 different penalty kicks.

Statistical comparison of pre- and post-training performance scores showed significant improvements for the experimental group as opposed to a control group. The improvement in performance was due to an improvement across all response categories. It appeared, therefore, that the film-based training programme improved anticipation performance. Given this type of training rarely occurs in practice, this was considered to be of practical significance.

The Non-kicking Foot

The research carried out by Dr Williams in the late 1980s was recently added to by the Canadian researchers referred to a little earlier. Their findings are not happy reading for the world's great goalkeepers.

As we've seen, of the 138 penalties taken in the four World Cups considered, 8 per cent were missed and 14.5 per cent were saved. Correct prediction of shot direction was achieved on only 41 per cent of all shots. Moving before the ball was kicked (against the laws of the game at all these tournaments) seems only to have made matters worse. Keepers moved early on 64 shots (46 per cent) and yet guessed correctly on only 25 of these shots. This research seemed to confirm what many observers and commentators have long said: namely, that moving too early is a poor strategy. It is critical to identify a reliable response cue that allows time to predict and respond accurately.

Franks and Harvey identified the following 'cues' in chronological order. The penalty taker's:

- Starting position.
- Angle of approach to the ball.

- Forward or backward lean of the trunk.
- Placement of the non-kicking foot.
- Inward or outward knee rotation of the kicking leg just prior to contact.
- Point of contact with the ball.

As you would probably expect, the later the response cue, the more accurate the prediction, and vice versa. Starting position and angle of run-up both fell below acceptable limits of reliability (set at 80 per cent accuracy). Point of ball contact was close to 98 per cent accurate, but if a keeper waits for this cue before starting to move he risks being too late. The same was found for the 'knee rotation of the kicking leg'.

The researchers found the only cue that was both reliable and time efficient was the placement of the non-kicking foot. It seems the position of the non-kicking foot dictates the direction of the shot. If the foot is directed towards the right, the shot will go towards the kicker's right, and vice versa. On the few occasions when the foot was pointing towards the centre of the goal, two outcomes seem most likely: either the ball is driven straight down the middle, or it is sliced to the right.

This cue was found to be 80 per cent reliable. A further test of the reliability of the cue was carried out on the penalties in Euro '96, with an accuracy of shot prediction of over 85 per cent. However, there is one big drawback: it only allows keepers between 150 and 200 milliseconds to react after detection.

Having identified the most relevant cue, the researchers went on to test its usefulness. They wanted to see whether it would be worth developing a training programme for keepers based upon its use. The key conclusions can be summarized as follows:

- An experimental group of soccer coaches and players, but no keepers, were able to improve their prediction accuracy up to

77 per cent having been given information about the non-kicking foot.
- However, reaction time for the group decreased as a consequence of searching for, and using, the relevant cue.
- Before the cue can be used effectively by goalkeepers, a training programme needs to be devised to reduce the time identifying the cue and the time taken to respond to it. Reaction times in the order of 200–300 milliseconds will not be fast enough to stop a penalty and have to be brought down to levels between 100–200 milliseconds.
- The non-kicking-foot cue only helps predict direction, it does not assist in predicting the height of the shot.

Despite these problems, Franks and Harvey remain confident that, given the appropriate training and adequate practice, goalkeepers can significantly improve their ability at stopping penalty kicks.

Some of you may be thinking at this point: 'What a load of bollocks. In a split second a goalkeeper is supposed to analyse the angle of run-up, angle of foot and hip, lean of trunk, direction of the non-kicking foot, the initial trajectory of the ball, oh yeah, having first consulted his computer, and then dive. Get real.'

But keepers of whatever standard do all these things already (except maybe the computer bit). The crucial thing is that more experienced keepers do them quicker, more instinctively, and more accurately. Sure, they have a huge advantage – they do nothing else but play football. The point is, and this applies to all keepers, the ability to guess the direction of a ball can be enhanced without actually having to face hundreds of penalties. Like anything, practice makes perfect, and a combination of video-training, real practice and analysis of potential opponents surely makes sense.

To Move or Not to Move . . . Revisited

I've just watched a fair few Scottish matches on television while holidaying in the Highlands in the summer of 1997. One game in particular was very instructive as far as guessing where the penalty was going, and also in respect of the optimum approach for a goalkeeper. The match between Celtic and Dunfermline on 16 August 1997 was won by Dunfermline, 2–1, much to the disgust of the Celtic faithful, who left early in their droves and roundly and deservedly booed their team off the field. The winning goal, and Celtic's goal, were both penalties, both converted with ease. Both goalkeepers moved so early that even I could have scored. Both had time to watch as the ball was calmly placed in the opposite corner.

What is it with keepers that so many persist in moving miles before the ball is kicked? How many times do we hear commentators, when talking about one-on-one situations in open play, stress the need for the keeper to 'make himself big' and not commit himself until the very last moment? Ian Wright, from *Inside Wright*: 'In a match, I am always looking for an opportunity to go one-on-one with the goalkeeper . . . I wait until the very last moment. I have in my mind to put the chance to the goalkeeper's left, because if he is right-handed it will take him longer to get down on that side. If the goalkeeper dives one way before I'm ready to shoot, it just makes my choice easier because I then put the ball in the other corner.'

Well, it should be the same for penalties. You may get lucky with an inexperienced penalty taker with the move-early technique, but the good to great takers will have you for breakfast. Why make it any easier for the taker? Don't forget, he's nervous too, and you need to try to make him feel even more insecure, to try to turn the psychological tables. Listen to this. Laurent Blanc of France, after he had scored the winning penalty for France in the quarter-final shoot-out against

Holland in Euro '96, admitted he had missed an important penalty before (in the Final of the French Cup) and that he had been in a state of terror when he walked up to take the kick: 'I had no idea where I was going to put my kick. I only made my mind up when I saw the goalkeeper move.'

Sadly, I cannot guarantee this guide will mean you automatically become a great penalty saver – I am afraid some God-given talent is also required. However, together with a lot of practice, it may help even-up the odds a little.

In *Coaching Modern Soccer Defence*, Eric G. Batty writes: 'While the keeper should practise at facing penalties, a note of caution should be sounded. Because penalty-taking is very much a matter of self-confidence, the one or two players who take them in matches should never be asked to give the goalkeeper practice. If he faces penalties taken by the same player over and over again, he will become familiar with the style of the kicker, and inevitably begin to save more shots. This will clearly have an adverse effect on the confidence of the penalty taker. Let other players therefore give the goalkeeper the practice he needs.'

How a goalkeeper should face up to a penalty in match-play depends very much on his personality and experience. Generally, though, there are only two courses of action open to him: a. to wait, nicely balanced to go either way, with his arms spread out at waist height, hands halfway down, and try to save the shot; b. to go one way and hope that he has guessed right.

If the coach knows something of the style of the opposition's usual penalty taker he should advise his goalkeeper before the match whether to expect a bombing hard-hit shot, or one that goes for accuracy; and, of course, tell him the side the penalty taker prefers, if he knows which it is.

The goalkeeper has to make an on-the-spot decision. The coach can only give him general advice. If a shot like a rocket is expected, or if the kicker turns out to be the centre-forward, big and strong with a long run-up to the ball, it is probably as well to wait and see. Many penalties I have seen, hit with real power straight at the middle of the goal, were certainly of a kind that could have been saved if the goalkeeper had not moved. On the other hand, a fierce shot, hit high into one of the corners, gives the goalkeeper little chance anyway; so, on balance, perhaps the best advice is to wait.

If the opponent taking the penalty is an accurate kicker and known to favour one side or the other, then it may be advisable for the goalkeeper to move to that side *as the kick is taken*. Conceivably, this might persuade the kicker to place the ball wide of the goalkeeper – too wide, as it may well prove. Or it might put him in two minds – and that can be equally fatal. There is a chance, of course, that the goalkeeper will go the wrong way, but a good goalkeeper who has faced this man before or has been told about him by his coach can add to the information he already possesses by looking for clues while he is waiting on the line. A short run-up, of only one or two steps, will indicate that the kicker has accuracy rather than power in mind; his angle of approach will suggest one side or the other. Of course a good player may make deliberate feints and in these conditions the goalkeeper is probably best advised to go for the corner that the kicker is known to favour, unless there are positive signs to the contrary.

8 – Referees

'Last time we got a penalty away from home, Christ was still a carpenter.' **Lenny Lawrence**

There is one person who can never get it right when it comes to a penalty: the ref. Referees always end up annoying someone.

Who can forget George Weah's unbelievable goal for AC Milan in 1997? Picking up a loose ball on the edge of his own area, he dribbled to the opposing team's penalty area, beating player after player before drilling it past the keeper. Pelé scored a similar goal in 1965.

Now imagine the same goal but just as Weah or Pelé is about to shoot – from well within the penalty area – one of the defenders rugby tackles him. I firmly believe some of the defending team's fans would still shout some abuse at the referee when he awards the penalty. Even sadder, some defenders would probably remonstrate with the referee about a penalty being awarded at all.

Now imagine another striker. Not George Weah, you can choose your own favourite here. He's sprung the offside trap and is just outside the penalty area with only the keeper to beat when he trips over his own feet. There is no other player within five yards of him. He falls to the ground as if shot, while at the same time ensuring he ends up in the penalty area, and screams for a penalty. He and his team-mates go berserk when the referee waves play on or, hopefully, books him for play-acting.

Silly examples? Sadly, and without naming names, we all know these examples are not so far removed from reality. And the man in the middle of all this 'professionalism run riot', the man who bears the brunt of all the abuse, the man who can change the course of a game, a championship or tournament with one decision, the man who can cost a club millions with just one blow of his whistle? The humble, and very poorly paid, referee.

You Are the Referee

Penalty decisions are always easy from the stands or with the benefit of super-slow-motion replays. It's not so straightforward when you have to call it as it happens.

You are the referee. It is an important English Division One game in November 1972. The date is relevant because the law is slightly different now, but even younger readers should be able to have a guess at the answer.

You have given a free-kick just inside the defending side's half. Defenders and attackers are moving to the edge of the penalty area in readiness for a long ball into the box. As the players are taking up their positions, before you blow for the kick to be taken and before it actually is taken, one of the attackers says something to one of the defenders. The defender elbows the attacker in the face. Both players are in the box.

You, all the players and the crowd see the whole thing. You immediately send the defender off but the attacking players and their fans all shout for a penalty. What do you do?

This is not a sample question from some referees' exam.

This situation really happened in a match between Crystal Palace and Everton, at Selhurst Park on 4 November 1972.

The referee, Norman Burtenshaw, gave the free-kick against Palace and then watched very carefully as the players moved to the edge of the Palace penalty area. In particular he was watching Alan Whittle, Everton's Under-23 International, and the Palace defender, Mel Blyth. He had an inkling something might happen. Sure enough, Whittle said something to Blyth as they ran back, whereupon Blyth elbowed Whittle in the face. The referee ordered Blyth off the field but the Everton players appealed for a penalty.

A clear penalty, surely? Elbowing someone in the face in the penalty area is about as clear-cut a penalty offence as you can get. You would be right, save for one thing – the ball was dead. The referee hadn't blown for the free-kick to be taken and, applying the current law for a moment, the ball had not been kicked. The ball was not in play, and if the ball was not in play the referee could not award a penalty. Sometimes it's no fun being a referee, particularly when you do not have a radio microphone which would allow you to explain such decisions to the crowd.

Inside or Out?

'It was a fair decision, the penalty, even though it was debatable whether it was outside or inside the box.' This quote was allegedly made by Sir Bobby Charlton, as recorded by someone for *Private Eye*'s 'Colemanballs'. It neatly sums up how the most difficult decision a referee has to make when it comes to awarding or refusing a penalty is, seemingly, pretty simple. Was the offence committed in the penalty area?

The laws are very specific with regard to location. It is the place where the offence is 'effective' which is the critical factor. If you are standing in the penalty area and hold your hand outside of the area and touch the ball, it is not a penalty. You have actually handled the ball outside the box even though you are standing in it. This is a difficult area for referees, because unless they are superhuman they can never always be in the optimum position to make such a call. Being any distance away can lead to a misjudgement. Take this example from twenty-five years ago: in 1973, Chelsea were playing Arsenal in an FA Cup quarter-final replay at Highbury. Five minutes before half-time Steve Kember brought George Armstrong down on the right-hand side of the pitch. The referee (Norman Burtenshaw again) thought the offence was outside the area and gave a free-kick just on the edge. The Arsenal players went crazy and surrounded the referee. Burtenshaw was renowned for never changing his mind once he'd made a decision. Nor did he feel it necessary to speak to the linesman, but somehow the Arsenal players persuaded him. Burtenshaw went over to the touchline and spoke to the linesman, Jack Griffiths, who confirmed the foul was inside the box and that it was a penalty.

In eleven years Burtenshaw had never changed a decision, but he did this time. The Chelsea players were furious. Alan Ball duly converted the penalty and Arsenal won the replay. When Burtenshaw saw the television footage of the incident the next day he was amazed – and relieved – the players had been at least a yard inside the box.

Referees apply their own 'severity' rule to make sense of the penalty law. If they see a mild foul in the box they often ignore it. One famous ref, Arthur Ellis, said of this: 'When [referees] should have awarded penalties they have taken the easy way out and given, instead, an indirect free-kick, or worse still, in shirking the main issue they have brought the ball outside the penalty area and ordered a free-kick from there. It happens. Players know it. Managers know it. The fans we might sometimes underestimate know it, and the guilty referees know it.'

Controversy has raged over many penalty kicks. A more bizarre instance occurred in a Crystal Palace match against Arsenal at Selhurst Park in 1972. Charlie George took a penalty and Palace's young reserve goalkeeper Paul Hammond pushed the ball on to the post and it rebounded, ran off his back and seemingly over the line, where Hammond grabbed it and pulled it back. The linesman signalled a goal and the referee pointed to the centre. *The Big Match* showed the incident over and over but they couldn't prove whether the ball was over the line because their camera was at the wrong angle.

Self-protection

This is an extract from a lecture given by Sir Stanley Rous in 1969:

> Referees are basically honest and impartial, but they do react differently to situations. How many referees will give a penalty against the home team early in a match, when play is often most fierce? We have all seen indirect free-kicks given in the penalty area instead of a penalty kick for one of the nine penalty offences. We have all seen referees whistle for penalty offences inside the area, then place the ball a foot or so outside the area. Thus degrees of punishment, instead of correct disciplinary action, are being applied . . .
>
> In an international tournament recently, I saw a referee give a penalty – in my view a harsh decision. The players, including the goalkeeper, took up proper positions without appeal, and the player taking the kick shot the ball straight into the goalkeeper's hands. He was ordered to retake the kick and scored – an absolute gift from the referee! At the 'inquest', the referee said that *he* was not ready for the kick to be taken and that he had not blown his whistle. At a European referees'

conference some years back, when I was making the point that an offence must be punished, regardless of the score and at any time in the match, I was shocked when one of the most famous and experienced referees of the time said, 'That's all very well, but I would never give a penalty against Austria in Vienna during the last few minutes of a match – and hope to get away safely!' The younger referees present were astonished at this confession.

Two further examples from the career of Norman Burtenshaw serve to illustrate the dangers of being a referee. In April 1972, Burtenshaw, one of the leading English referees of the time, had the honour/misfortune to be chosen to referee the second leg of a European Cup match between Ajax and Benfica. The match was held at the Stadium of Light in Lisbon, with Ajax leading 1–0 from the first leg.

Early on in the game, Burtenshaw made himself popular with the home team and fans by disallowing an Ajax goal. However, a few minutes later, the ball hit an Ajax player on the hand inside the penalty area. The referee did not consider the handball was deliberate and so waved play on. From a personal-safety point of view this was both brave and completely mad. Seventy thousand fanatical Benfica fans went berserk. Bottles, oranges and lemons cascaded down from the stands and on to the pitch. Some fans tried to rush on to the pitch but were held back by the police. Unfortunately, no one was holding back the police. An incensed policeman advanced on Burtenshaw with his police baton raised shouting, 'Handball.' Thankfully, he was dragged away by his colleagues before things got ugly. After the game, Burtenshaw received a 19-carat-gold whistle and a brooch.

Later the same year Burtenshaw was refereeing a match in South Africa between Kaiser Chiefs and Orlando Pirates in Soweto. He gave a penalty against the home side, who lost 2–0. The crowd rioted, a stand roof collapsed, killing one man, and two youths were knifed. In the early days of South African soccer, the ref's life was often in serious danger. If the home team failed to win, the ref often had to be smuggled out in disguise – as a policeman or a woman – to avoid the angry crowds waiting to lynch him. Some frightened refs went on to the field armed – one once produced a cut-throat razor to protect himself from players angry with a decision.

George Best is sent off by Norman Burtenshaw, August 1971

On one occasion when a referee dismissed Pelé from the field for dissent, the crowd stormed the pitch. The police just saved the ref's life and he was taken away, with one of the linesmen taking over. The crowd refused to allow the match to continue until Pelé was returned to the field. This occurred in Columbia.

Some Controversial Penalty Decisions/Incidents Involving Referees

- With his Brazilian side San Lorenzo 2–1 up over Estudiantes in the final minutes of a league fixture, defender Siminiola picked up the ball thinking it had already gone out of play. To his amazement the referee, Humberto Dellacasa, awarded a penalty. The spot kick was converted and two players were sent-off for manhandling the referee, who had to be escorted from the pitch by riot police.

- In October 1997, referee Martin Bradford-Brown abandoned a match he was refereeing when a player exposed his private parts to him with the McDonald's-inspired comment: 'If that's a penalty I suppose you think this banana is a Big Mac.'

- The introduction of the goal-net required a referee to be beaten up first. Scot, John Brodie, a staunch Everton fan, was persuaded by a friend to watch an amateur Cup game the friend was refereeing in 1890. The friend disallowed two seemingly good goals and the crowd beat him up. The next day, Brodie went to the Post Office and took out a provisional patent on goal-nets. A year later, when the patent came up for renewal, a sports outfitters in London paid him £100 for the idea – bizarrely, he gave the money to Everton. Nets were used for the first time in a match between Nottingham Forest and Bolton Wanderers in 1891.

- In the third round of the FA Cup in 1900–01 Spurs were having a hard time against Reading (1–1) when their keeper made a parry and left-back Sandy Tait prevented a certain goal by punching the ball out from under the bar. Despite protests, the ref gave a goal kick – Spurs won the replay 3–0 and went on to become the last non-League team to win the Cup.

- Fifteen minutes from the end of the Irish Cup Final in 1899, Linfield were beating Glentoran 1–0 when one of their defenders punched the ball away from an open goal. Clear as day, but the ref didn't give it, whereupon the Glentoran team walked off the field, forfeiting the Cup.

- In the 1994 World Cup finals, Kurt Rothlisberger was sent back to Switzerland after admitting he should have given Belgium a penalty against the holders Germany, following Thomas Helmer's foul on Josip Weber. Germany won 3–2 to reach the quarter-final.

- Argentina were going for a hat-trick of South American Championships in 1995, and were leading 2–1 in the quarter-final against Brazil. With ten minutes left Jorginho's low cross into the box was knocked in by Tulio Pereira – clearly using his hands. The goal was allowed and Brazil won on penalties. Divine retribution – Tulio put Brazil up in the Final against Uruguay and then was the only player to miss in the shoot-out which decided the Final.

- The only goal of the Heysel disaster Final was a Platini penalty, given for a foul on Boniek by Gillespie. Not only was it not a foul, but it was also outside the box.

- In Euro '96, Nieto, the ref in the France–Holland quarter-final gave Holland a free-kick for handball even though the offence was clearly in the box. Then, in the penalty shoot-out he insisted on replacing the ball just as Seedorf was preparing to take his kick – Seedorf was the only player to miss.

- Switzerland have probably suffered the most dodgy refereeing decisions in a short space of time – on their tour of Africa in 1983. They lost to Zimbabwe having twice gone ahead but having been pegged back each time by a penalty. Against Kenya they had three clear penalties turned down. Finally, against the Ivory Coast, they lost to a late penalty after their own defender had been fouled. What was even worse was the local groundsman had painted the penalty spots two yards too close to the goal.

- In February 1996, Lazio's Beppe Signori converted a very late penalty to beat Roma in the local derby and then ran off to celebrate with the Lazio fans . . . which earned him his second booking of the match. He was sent off.

- In the first ever Scottish Cup Final, James J. Lang scored a goal for Clydesdale but the ref/umpire, James McIntyre, thought it offside. The only problem was the officials could only disallow a goal if the defending side appealed, and Queen's Park hadn't apppealed. So McIntyre apparently muttered under his breath that they should have said something – whereupon, surprise, surprise, someone appealed, the goal was disallowed and Queen's Park won 2–0.

Epilogue

by James Miller

It is with a very deep sadness that I, the author's father, am writing the Epilogue to this book. Clark died suddenly, before he had time to add the finishing touches, including Chapter 9, where he intended to discuss the future of the penalty kick.

His final intention was to circulate a questionnaire to a wide cross-section of the public involved with football. This was to include players, managers, coaches, associations and journalists. And not least of all, football fans. Unfortunately, Clark missed the last post.

Being a great football fan himself, he was well aware that any future decision on the way to end drawn games must consider the views of the fans. Clark knew that fans want to see fair play, a competitive finish, and for the best team to win. He never lost sight of the fact that true football fans must be allowed to voice, in their inimitable style, their own views. He believed that any future decision coming from the football authorities must be made in consultation with the true fans:

those folk who spend, week in week out, hard-earned cash to support their beloved team. At the end of the day the fans are the game's lifeline and should have a role in any decision-making process.

At the time of writing, FIFA's current preferred solution for the 1998 World Cup in France is, after a drawn game at full time, extra-time then the first goal deciding the result – the Golden Goal or sudden death. If the game is still drawn at the end of extra-time, penalties will be then taken by each team to determine the result.

This solution has many supporters but it remains to be seen if this outcome satisfies the players and the fans.

We will reserve judgement.

The Way Forward

Clark, as you will already be aware, was a big fan of the penalty shoot-out. He took the view that penalty takers and goalkeepers should be coached and practise to a level where guessing is removed from the equation and they rely on their own skills.

Stress is a strange emotion and affects us all in different ways. We have all experienced stress in our everyday lives. Too much stress and anxiety seriously affects our ability to focus on our skills and affects our performance. We are all responsible for our own stress levels, but we can control them.

How do we control, or more to the point, how does a penalty taker and goalkeeper control, stress and anxiety?

I am certain that the author's scientific approach to penalty-kicking and goalkeeping is the way forward and, if followed, would reduce stress and anxiety and, more importantly, feelings of guilt.

My son and I had many talks on this particular point. In fact, our talks probably motivated him to do the research for this book. And it was pressure from Clark's 5-year-old daughter, Ella, which provided the incentive to complete the project. His opinion, and I concur, was: there is a correct way to take a penalty, and a correct way to try to save it.

Let me explain his thinking: a penalty taker has a favoured striking foot. Very few players are actually strong with both feet, and a penalty taker will favour his striking foot when kicking the ball. (I can hear you say, 'Well, that's pretty obvious.')

Now, a first-class player, when approaching the kick, will look at the goal and decide where he is going to direct the ball. He may have another look, but does not look again if he is worth his salt. His eye has recorded to his brain exactly where he is going to put the ball, both in relation to the goalposts and the goalkeeper. His eyes are now on the ball right up to the point of contact (keep your head down and your eye on the ball).

You will now remember the scientific analysis in Chapter 7. The main point to be picked up here is for the goalkeeper – that last look at goal should be where the kick will be directed. Too easy? What if the taker bluffs and changes his mind? Yes, he can change his mind, but if he does so, he stands a very good chance of misdirecting his kick. Watch the next penalty taken on television and see if the author has got it right. But do watch an expert – Dennis Bergkamp or Alan Shearer.

I mentioned earlier the favoured striking foot. A right-footed player should favour placing the ball (by placing I mean not blasting) to his right, or the goalkeeper's left. On the other hand, if he is going to blast it, he will generally do so to the left of the goal, the goalkeeper's right side. The opposite scenario holds for a left-footed penalty taker.

Therefore, we have another clue for the goalkeeper. Tie this in with the details on body-language and kicking angles, and much of the guessing should be taken out of the equation for goalkeepers. Still no guarantee for a save, but a considerable help.

Now to goalkeepers. It is frequently said that goalkeepers have a favourite side when diving. The author and I discussed this point at some length, but we did not come to a firm conclusion.

Our talks revolved around the goalkeeper being right- or left-handed, and this affecting his favoured diving side. For example, a right-handed goalkeeper would favour diving to his own left; a left-handed keeper would favour diving to his own right. In effect they would get down, or across, quicker to their favoured side.

A clue for penalty takers?

As I said, we came to no firm conclusion on this point. Why not resolve this issue for us?

The next time you are out on the pitch with a ball, see if you have a favoured side for diving and relate it to your left or right hand. You never know – perhaps you will be able to settle this issue without a scientific experiment.

Clark was firmly convinced that an intelligent and considered approach to penalty-taking, both from the taker's and the keeper's viewpoint, must be the way forward (i.e., no guessing).

Stress and anxiety can be kept under control by a practised approach to the task in hand. Do your homework, practise accordingly, and confidence will be raised, whilst stress levels and anxiety should be kept low.

My son considered the penalty shoot-out in its present form a fair way to end a drawn game. He did accept, however, that many fans found the shoot-out unacceptable and unfair to their team.

He has attempted in his book to put his preferred solution into perspective and proposed that a little-known clause in the penalty shoot-out rules could be used to get round that unacceptable and unfair tag.

I now quote this clause in full:

- A penalty shoot-out forms no part of the match itself. It is simply a mechanism to decide which team progresses to the next round or wins a tournament. The match itself is recorded as a draw.

The author suggested that the above clause could be used as a solution, and I will quote him in full:

- You can play for penalties if you want to, but any tournament actually won after a shoot-out will be deemed a draw. Sure, the Cup will go to the winners of the shoot-out, but each team will receive exactly the same medal – a Drawers' medal – there will be no winners' or runners-up medals. Prize money will be reduced if the tournament is won on penalties. There will be no winners' prize money; the two Finalists will share the runners-up money.

As an aside, I would like to mention an earlier suggestion from Ernie Walker, chairman of the Scottish Football Independent Review Commission. In conversation with the author he said that he liked the shoot-out but disliked them being called penalties. No foul has been committed and he preferred the term 'kicks from the penalty spot'. He further suggested that these kicks should take place from the 18-yard line and be taken from a point on the line the taker chooses. The keeper can move, charge out – whatever. And the taker has to beat him with one shot.

The intention is to change the emphasis to one of success. Fewer goals will be scored and one goal will win the match. Rather than a miss losing it. He would also stop the shoot-out as soon as one team goes ahead after an equal number of kicks. Ernie would also like to widen and increase the height of the goal.

I include Ernie Walker's comments at this stage of our conclusion mainly to emphasize that there is still a great debate going on out there. The solution has still to be found and needs further discussion.

My attempt to gather together my son's book does not do the author justice. He had a wealth of detail and comments from many people in the UK and abroad, together with statistics, photographs and match reports. I can only appeal to readers to perhaps help continue the debate.

I have included Clark's own questionnaire, in fact, one returned to him by Alan Shearer (see Appendix 2). It was his intention to circulate these questions to the wide footballing fraternity – including the fans.

I am sure the author would be happy in knowing that you are all interested in finding a sensible solution. Could you find the time to fill in the questionnaire? I don't have an address for my son – at least not yet. So perhaps you could send your reply direct to the FA or FIFA – my son would chuckle at the thought.

And, finally, it was the author's intention to pay a visit to Northern Ireland – in particular to Milford, in County Armagh. William McCrum is buried there, and Clark wanted to visit his grave, read his obituary and pay his respects. It all started with this Irish goalkeeper and my son had developed a great liking for the man and his legacy. His obituary notice is printed on the next two pages.

William McCrum (middle row, second from left)

Armagh's Great Loss

Passing of Mr. W. McCrum
It is with sincere regret we record the death of a brilliant scholar, raconteur and renowned sportsman, in the person of Mr Wm. McCrum, J.P.

Mr McCrum, whose name will be forever associated with Milford, was in failing health for some time past and had a seizure on Tuesday which necessitated his removal to Armagh County Infirmary, where he succumed on Wednesday.

Mr McCrum was a son of the late Mr R. G. McCrum, D.L., Milford, ex-High Sheriff for County Armagh and for a number of years Chairman of Armagh County Council.

Deceased, who was educated at Armagh Royal School and Trinity College, Dublin, had a brilliant academic career, was extremely well read, a brilliant raconteur, and was the author of some very meritorious sketches.

He was one of the old Town Commissioners and an enthusiastic member of the Armagh Bohemian Club (now extinct). Of later years he was a member of the County Club, English Street. He was also a member of the Board of Governors of Armagh Royal School.

In business circles he was extremely well known, and for a number of years represented the firm of Messrs McCrum, Watson & Mercer, linen manufacturers, in London. Quite recently he retired from business and went to reside in England, but his heart was in Armagh and he returned to the Primatial City.

He always evinced a keen interest in the Boy Scout movement, and was Ulster Commissioner of that organisation for a considerable number of years.

Mr McCrum, who was a brother of Mrs Miller, J.P., Drumsill, has a son, Commander C. McCrum, who occupies a high position in the Royal Navy, and who commanded H.M.S. Hood when the warship visited Bangor in the spring of this year.

An All Round Sportsman

Although Mr McCrum was well known in social and commercial life, it was, however, in sports circles that he was perhaps best known, as he was a leading figure in the cricket world and had been a prominent figure in the football world. A member of the Northern Cricket Union, he was instrumental in forming the Milford Cricket Club, and to his coaching may be attributed the many successes of the club. He also was particularly interested in the affairs of the Armagh Cricket Club, and since Milford discontinued participating in competitive cricket he never missed a match in which the Armagh Club was engaged. He was the mentor of several youngsters who showed latent cricket ability, and during the summer months was to be frequently seen on the Mall coaching his protegees in the art of wielding the willow. He was also connected with Armagh Rugby Football Club.

A Member of the I.F.A.

Mr McCrum was directly responsible for a very important alteration made in the laws of Association football, viz., the penalty kick rule. Mr McCrum, who was for a time a member of the I.F.A. and goalkeeper for Milford F.C., County Armagh, was for many years deeply interested in Irish football, and particularly in the old Mid-Ulster Football Association, to which he presented a handsome silver challenge cup for competition by the Mid-Ulster clubs. In the year 1890 Mr McCrum submitted a draft of the penalty kick to Mr J. Reid, secretary of the Association, who placed it before the Committee of the Irish Football Association for permission to send it forward to the coming meeting of the International Football Board. The I.F.A. decided to send in the proposal for inclusion in the laws of the game. Its appearance in the Press aroused a perfect storm of ridicule on the question. One paper described it as the 'Irishman's Motion', another that it would turn the playing field into a 'gridiron'. The amateur section were of opinion no player would deliberately kick an opponent.

At the meeting of the International Board, held in Anderson's Hotel, London, in June, 1890, the Irish representative agreed to withdraw the motion, if it was subsequently discussed. This course was adopted. After discussion the Board passed a resolution, 'That the Board is desirable of legislation on these lines,' and adjourned the question until next meeting. The following year, at the Alexandra Hotel, Glasgow, Mr J. Reid, I.F.A. secretary, proposed, and Mr Chas Crump, F.A., seconded, the penalty kick rule – No. 13 in the laws of the game – when it was passed unanimously. Thus to Mr Wm. McCrum belongs the credit of inventing the original penalty kick rule.

Armagh mourns the loss of one who was so highly esteemed and respected by all creeds and classes. It is, however, to Milford that the severest blow comes, for it may be truly stated that he was loved by the inhabitants of the village, in whose welfare he always took a fatherly interest.

To his relatives we tender our heartfelt sympathy in the irreparable loss they have sustained.

AN APPRECIATION

(By 'Mid-On',who contributes Cricket Notes to the 'Ulster Gazette'.)

It is with difficulty I bring myself to write of the passing of one with whom I was intimately acquainted. Mr McCrum, who was a recognised authority on the rules of cricket, frequently contributed to my notes, and his store of knowledge as regards matters connected with the game was always at my disposal. He was the backbone of both the Armagh and Milford clubs, and his passing leaves a gap which can never be filled. He took a practical interest in the education of promising youngsters from a cricket point of view, and the results of his tuition will be apparent in local cricket for years to come. On behalf of all the local cricketers and myself I tender to the relatives sincere sympathy in their sad bereavement. The moral lessons of the great game were always evident in his life, for he never did anything that wasn't 'cricket'.

Information supplied by Andrew Crozier, Milford, N. Ireland

I hope this book stands as a tribute to William McCrum and his footballing legacy, and to the author, Clark Miller.

James Miller, April 1998

Appendix 1

Curios . . . Awards . . . and Other Things

- Eric Viscaal, a Belgian outfield player, was forced to take over in goal in the AA Ghent v Lokeren fixture in 1994 when Ghent's keeper was sent off in the last few minutes. His first act was to save a penalty, and then, with seconds to go, Ghent were awarded a penalty, and he went up the other end and scored.
- Up to the start of the 1997–98 season, only two players have missed penalties in League Cup Finals at Wembley – Clive Walker for Sunderland missed in 1985, and Nigel Winterburn of Arsenal had his saved by Luton's Andy Dibble in 1988.
- Aston Villa's Ray Graydon also had his penalty saved by Norwich's Kevin Keelan in the 1975 Final, but he scored from the rebound.
- Andy Blair set a League Cup record when he scored a hat-trick of penalties for Sheffield Wednesday against Luton in the fourth round on 20 November, 1984.
- Jan Molby's first hat-trick in English football all came from the penalty spot in Liverpool's 3–1 win over Coventry in November 1986.
- Arthur Birch scored five goals for Chesterfield in the 1923–24 season – as a goalkeeper. All came from the penalty spot.

- Ian Dunn was the first player in British football to settle a match with a Golden Goal when he scored in the 107th minute to seal Huddersfield's win over Lincoln in an Auto-Windscreens Shield tie.
- Jan Tomaszewski, Poland's goalkeeper in the 1974 World Cup finals, became the first man to save two penalties in the same tournament.
- Johan Neeskens scored the fastest goal in a World Cup Final when he scored a penalty for Holland after only two minutes. The first West German player to touch the ball was Sepp Maier, when he picked it out of the net.
- There has been only one goalless draw in a World Cup Final – the 1994 Final was decided on penalties.
- Kazimieriz Deyma played his 100th game for Poland in the 1978 finals but missed a penalty against Argentina in a 2–0 defeat.
- Only three times in the history of FA Cup Finals has a penalty been the only goal of the game: Huddersfield beat Preston in 1922; Preston beat Huddersfield in 1938; and Tottenham won a replay against QPR in 1982.
- Charlie Wallace of Aston Villa was the first person to miss a penalty in an FA Cup Final when he missed in the 1913 Final.
- The first FA Cup match to be decided by penalties was the 1972 'third place play-off' between Birmingham City and Stoke City – the Blues won 4–3.
- The first Wembley Final to be decided on a Golden Goal was the 1995 Auto-Windscreens Shield. Paul Tait's goal in the 103rd minute ensured Birmingham beat Carlisle 1–0.
- The away-goal rule for European competitions was first introduced in 1967. It didn't replace the replay but was designed to alleviate the problem.
- In 1924 Cardiff City had the opportunity to become the first and only Welsh club to win the Football League Championship. Needing a victory to take the title, City were

awarded a penalty in the final game for the season against Birmingham. But Len Davies missed the kick and Huddersfield won the title on goal average.

- Southend finished bottom of the Third Division South in 1921–22, scoring only 34 goals. Their top scorer was a full-back, Jimmy Evans, whose 10 goals were all penalties.
- In the Mexico v Bulgaria 1994 World Cup penalty shoot-out: Jorge Campos, Mexico's keeper, guessed correctly on each shot but they were just too well hit – sadly, all bar one of his strikers missed. Otherwise in USA '94, the penalties, including shoot-outs, were almost exclusively characterized by keepers moving too early, and being passed the other side. The evidence is compelling – to move early doesn't help. Standing your ground until absolutely the last second gives you the chance to save the shot down the middle and the badly hit shot, and still gives you the chance to use all the anticipatory cues and dive correctly. Keepers should be turning the tables on takers – the psychological advantage needs to be wrested from the penalty takers – once that happens, then you will automatically increase your chances of saving, because a player nervous about missing is far more likely to do just that.
- When Scotland reached the European Championship finals for the first time in 1992, they owed it, in the end and paradoxically, to the brilliant Gheorghe Hagi. After the Scots failed to score enough goals against San Marino at home, Romania needed to win at home against Bulgaria, and score at least twice, to pip Scotland to the one qualifying place.

  Romania took the lead after half an hour, but Adrian Popescu's goal should have been the clincher: earlier Hagi had hit a penalty straight at Borislav Mikhailov. If he'd scored, Romania would have won 2–1 and reached the finals; instead, the eventual 1–1 draw sent Scotland through.

Irony here, because when the Scots were sailing through the group they were pulled up by a 1–0 defeat in Romania, whose goal was scored by Hagi – from the penalty spot.

- 1988 saw the first major shoot-out in Scotland, in the Scottish League Cup. Aberdeen beat Rangers 5–3 on penalties.
- The May 1990 Scottish Cup Final – between Celtic and Aberdeen saw 120 minutes of dire football and then a shoot-out. It took 20 minutes: Celtic missed their first kick; Aberdeen their fourth. With 18 kicks taken neither keeper had yet touched the ball. Aberdeen's tenth attempt by Anton Rogan was brilliantly saved by Theo Snelders and Brian Irvine scored for Celtic to win 9–8.
- Torquay become the first team to win promotion on penalties. A Fourth Division play-off against Blackpool was won 5–4 on penalties.
- On 9 August 1997, Motherwell played Inverness Caledonian Thistle in the Scottish Coca-Cola Cup. The score was 2–2 after extra-time, but Motherwell won 4–1 on penalties as Inverness' nerve failed. Steve Patterson, the Thistle manager, admitted that he only had three volunteers for the penalty shoot-out and two players whose shots were saved had to be pressed into taking the kicks. 'I am disappointed at going out on penalties, but last season we won two Cups in penalty shoot-outs, so I suppose things balance themselves out,' he said.
- Those who believe England has one domestic Cup too many can use the 1985 League Cup Final as ammunition; a throw-back to the early days when the leading sides didn't enter and the Rochdales and Rotherhams reached the Final. In this case, for the only time, two of the top division's relegated teams, Norwich and Sunderland, contested the Final.

The match, which had no trouble living down to its billing, turned on two incidents. First, Asa Hartford's low shot from the left hit Gordon Chisholm and went in at the near post. Then, only a minute later, Dennis Van Wijk handled in the area and Clive Walker, a flashy winger who'd scored against his old club in the semi-final at Stamford Bridge, hit the base of a post. Norwich, having lost two League Cup deciders by a single goal, won by the same margin. Sunderland have never won the trophy.

- After a disastrous first appearance in the World Cup finals (they lost 7–0 to Uruguay in 1954), Scotland didn't make much more of an impression four years later, a draw with Yugoslavia and defeat by Paraguay leaving them needing to beat France (Kopa, Fontaine and all) to reach the quarter-finals. They lost 2–1, but only after John Hewie, the tall South African full-back, had hit a post from the penalty spot. Scotland have never qualified for the second stage of any World Cup finals.
- A number of European club Finals have been decided by shoot-outs, but only the Barcelona team of 1986 missed every kick they took, four in all (their opponents Steaua Bucharest missed two; all six were saved), taken by Marcos (Alonso), captain José Ramon Alexanko, and two fallen Angels, Pedraza and 'Pichi' Alonso. Surprising that – because they'd won their semi-final on penalties.
- In 1978 Poland played their first World Cup second-round group match against the hosts Argentina, who'd had their share of luck in scraping through: two Hungarians sent off, a penalty wrongly awarded against France, defeat by Italy. Poland, no longer the dashing team that finished third in 1974, had been just as unimpressive.

Still, a goal down, they had a great chance of equalizing against Argentina. Their captain Kaziu Deyna took a free-kick, a scramble followed, and Mario Kempes (whose goal was dividing the teams) made another major contribution by handling on the line. Deyna, whose lame spot kick was easily saved by Ubaldo Fillol, was the only player to miss a penalty in his 100th international. He was not capped again after the tournament, which Argentina went on to win.

- The battle for the 1985–86 Bundesliga title went to the wire. With two matches left, Werder Bremen led the table by two points but had to play their nearest challengers Bayern Munich in the penultimate round. A win for Werder would give them the title, a draw would leave them two points clear (but with an inferior goal difference) with one match to play.

  There was no score with only two minutes left when they were awarded a penalty, which was taken by their central defender Michael Kutzop, who'd already converted seven spot kicks that season. This time he hit the post. Bayern escaped with a draw then won their last match 6–0, while Werder lost theirs 2–1 and missed the title on goal difference.
- At one stage of the 1993–94 season, Deportivo La Coruña led the Spanish First Division by seven points, but went into their last two games needing maximum points to win the title. A sturdy 2–0 away win over Logrones set them up for the decider at home to Valencia.

  On this final day, whilst nearest challengers Barcelona were recovering from 1–2 down to beat Sevilla 5–2, La Coruña were being held goalless in their Riazor stadium. Then, inside the last two minutes, they were awarded a penalty.

  The regular taker, Donato Gama da Silva, had been substituted, which left the responsibility to the Serbian sweeper Miroslav Djukic, one of the stars of their season. In front of 30,000 success-starved fans, his weak shot was easily saved by Jose Luis Gonzalez. Djukic fell to his knees in despair, and for the third season in a row Barcelona won the title thanks to a blunder by their closest rivals. Deportivo La Coruña have yet to win the Spanish league. The previous year, they'd finished third after topping the table for much of the season. In the game that turned the tide, away to Real Madrid, they lost 2–1 after leading 1–0 at half-time – and missing a penalty!

- In the first leg of the 1994–95 First Division play-offs, Stuart Lovell scored twice in Reading's 3–1 win at Tranmere, effectively ensuring a place in the play-off Final against Bolton.

  But at Wembley he missed the penalty that would have put Reading 3–0 ahead and almost certainly into the top division for the first time in their history. Later in the same match, he missed an easy chance, then lost the ball to let Bolton in for an equalizer with only seven minutes left. Reading lost 4–3 in extra-time.

  Forgiveness is divine, and sometimes Readingensian. Lovell was given a two-year contract, and the Elm Park fans called for him to take the next penalty at home the following season. He scored.
- After each team had won the home leg of the 1974 Libertadores Cup (South American equivalent of the European Cup), São Paulo of Brazil fought out a tense play-off with Independiente of Argentina, a match decided by two penalties; one scored by Independiente's Uruguayan defender Ricardo Pavoni, the other (which would have brought the equalizer) taken by Ze Carlos and saved by Carlos Alfredo Gay. São Paulo then had to wait a further eighteen years to win the Cup for the first time.
- Welsh fans look back on the relative golden years of 1974–76, when the national team reached the European Championship quarter-finals and came close to doing even better. But at Ninian Park, Josip Katalinski scored from a penalty, Terry Yorath missed another, and the 1–1 draw sent Yugoslavia through to the last four.
- Ajax won the European Cup three times in a row (1971–73) and might have challenged Bayern Munich in 1974 if they'd survived a tough opening tie against CSKA Sofia. In the first leg, the Dutch unveiled their new striker, the sharp and dangerous Jan Mulder, who'd scored twice and hit a post for Anderlecht in the 1970 Fairs Cup Final against Arsenal. He scored another here – but also missed a penalty, and the 1–0

win wasn't quite enough. Ajax lost the return 2–0 after extra-time.

- Despite losing the first leg of the 1973 European Cup semi-final 3–1 in Turin, Derby County had every chance of winning the tie at home, especially when 17-year-old Steve Powell put Alan Hinton clear in the second half. The winger ran into the penalty area, was brought down, and got up to take the kick himself. Normally a fierce and reliable penalty expert, he shot wide, the 0–0 draw sent Juventus through to the Final, and Derby have yet to progress as far again in Europe.
- The machinations of Italian clubs in European competition have been the subject of much speculation, to say the least. Ask Liverpool (1965), Derby and Leeds (1973) among others. A big subject, which has filled a book of its own.

  Space here for a couple of examples. When Juventus reached the 1965 Fairs Cup Final, they managed to have it played over a single leg – and have it held in their own stadium! They lost 1–0 to Ferencváros.

  In 1973, after they'd lost in the European Cup Final and Ajax refused to play in the World Club Cup, Juve were up to the same tricks, persuading Independiente to play just a single match for the title – in Rome.

  Again Juventus lost 1–0, but only after Antonello Cuccureddu, their nuggety defensive midfielder, had missed a penalty when the score was 0–0. A second helping of just deserts.
- Although a bad knee injury prevented Len Thompson from staking a regular place in the strong Arsenal team of the late 1920s, he did become the club's leading penalty taker. Indeed, before a game against Sheffield United, Highbury was festooned with placards announcing 'How I take penalty kicks, by Len Thompson', and action pictures of his technique.

  No prizes for guessing. Midway through the first half, Arsenal were awarded a penalty, the photographers lined up behind the United goal, and Thompson's kick nearly hit the corner flag.

- Jupp Heynckes scored a record five goals in UEFA Cup Finals, including the last hat-trick in any European Final (1975). Two years earlier, in the decider against Liverpool, he scored both goals in the 2–0 win the second leg – but if he'd converted a penalty in the first leg at Anfield, Borussia Mönchengladbach would have won on away goals. As it was, they lost 3–2 on aggregate.
- Hard to think of Tommy Hutchinson's long legs as the most natural tools for taking penalties, and so it proved in the European Championship qualifyer against Spain at Hampden in 1974.

  Scotland were leading 1–0 when the big Spanish stopper Mihueli handled in the area. Encouraged by Hutchinson's missed kick, Spain won 2–1, and Scotland didn't qualify for the finals until 1992.
- The penalty missed by John Machin against Charlton Athletic in September 1972 didn't affect promotion or relegation at the end of the season, but it cost York City the match – and set up a neat little coincidence.

  The kick was awarded for handball by Charlton's Vince O'Kane. Later in the game, O'Kane scored the only goal of the match, from a penalty given for handball – by Machin!
- In 1959, after winning the first three European Cups, Real Madrid faced a stiff challenge in the semi-final from the club on their own doorstep, Atlético Madrid, who were only 2–1 down in the away leg when they were awarded a penalty, which was taken by Eduardo Isidio Netto, better known as Vava, who'd scored twice for Brazil in the World Cup Final the previous year. He missed it (Ferenc Puskas had scored with one for Real), Atlético were beaten in a play-off and didn't reach the Final till 1974.
- In their very first European Cup match, in Belgium in 1956, Manchester United conceded an early penalty taken by the

Anderlecht captain, the classy striker Jef Mermans. He hit the post and was beaten to the rebound by Bill Foulkes, who cleared downfield for Dennis Violett to score. United won this first leg 2–0 – and the second 10–0!

- Before the match against Wales in 1902, England had scored in each of 52 consecutive internationals going back to 1884. Ernest Needham missed a penalty and the game was drawn 0–0, whereupon England scored in their next 32 matches – but for the Nudger's miss, this would have added up to a remarkable 85 in a row. As it was, that 52 was the world record before Hungary overhauled it in 1955. It was Needham's last penalty kick for England.
- When Carmel Busuttil had his penalty pushed on to the post in an international match in 1995, the earth didn't move. Clashes between Malta and Luxembourg don't register on the Richter scale. Still, it mattered to both of them, and not just because European Championship points were at stake.

  To the Maltese, it meant that Busuttil didn't add to his national record of 20 goals in internationals (14 ahead of the next on the list!). To the good burghers of Lux, Paul Kock's save, made in the last minute, showed an appropriate sense of occasion. It preserved a 1–0 win, which ended a run of exactly 80 internationals without a win, far and away the world record. It was Luxembourg's first victory against anyone since 1980, their first against a European side since 1973, and their first away from home since 1963!

  After that, like waiting for a bus, two more victories came along in brisk succession, against Malta again and the Czech Republic, no less.
- Roger Byrne was unlucky that the goalkeepers who faced the two penalties he took for England were among the best in the world: Gylmar dos Santos of Brazil and Vladimir Beara of Yugoslavia. Both saved his kicks, which didn't affect the results (England won 4–2 and 3–0) but made Byrne the only player never to score for England despite taking two penalties.

- Against Belgium in 1982, Kenny Dalglish had one of his few commanding games for Scotland, scoring two goals in Brussels: one breathtaking, the other merely marvellous. They put the Scots 2–1 up and seemed to have given them two European Championship points. Then, in the 78th minute, after Belgium had recovered to take the lead, Scotland were awarded a penalty for a trip by Jan Ceulemans on Graeme Souness.

  John Robertson, who took these kicks for Scotland and Nottingham Forest, was on the substitutes' bench, leaving the responsibility to left-back Frank Gray, whose confidence probably wasn't helped by the ball rolling off the spot. Jean-Marie Pfaff saved his shot, the 3–2 scoreline stood, and Scotland yet again didn't reach the finals.
- Two penalties were missed in the course of actual play in Euro '96. The first, by Scotland's captain Gary McAllister (the ball rolling off the spot again!), was the turning point of the match against England, who scored their second goal a minute later. The second, Gianfranco Zola's weak attempt against Germany, cost Italy not only a place in the quarter-finals, but (in view of how far the Czech Republic went) even greater things.

  Four years earlier, McAllister had scored for Scotland in their only win of the 1992 finals – from the penalty spot.
- How fitting that the 1994 World Cup finals should end with a missed penalty: they'd started with one.

  At the opening ceremony in Chicago, a ball was placed for a spot kick only a few yards from goal. Unmissable? Not for singer Diana Ross, whose links with football were proved to be as tenuous as we thought when she hooked the ball wide to the left. After that, the only way for the tournament was up.

  The following year, Ross opened another World Cup, this time the rugby league version at Wembley. She wasn't asked to take a kick at goal.

- Needing to win their last qualifying match, in Vienna, to reach the 1990 World Cup finals, East Germany saw their best chance disappear when Rico Steinmann missed a penalty – this after Austria had scored their second goal from the spot. It was East Germany's last competitive match as a separate nation.
- A number of FA Amateur Cup Finals were decided by penalty misses. Alan Bermingham's for Skelmersdale in 1967, for instance, and Kenny Kent's for Chesham in 1968.

  Back in 1915, centre-forward Hopper missed an early spot kick for the holders Bishop Auckland, just before Clapton scored the only goal of the game.

  In 1922, Bishop Auckland were again holders, but this time the boot was on the other foot, their goalkeeper Potts saving a penalty by South Bank right-back Thompson which would have given the outsiders a 3–2 lead. The Bishops won 5–2 after extra-time.

  Oh, and a player called Steward missed the penalty which would have equalized for Crook Town in the 1958 semi-final – after Ilford's Whittall had scored the only goal of the game from the spot.
- In the Home Championship match against England at Goodison Park in 1935, Northern Ireland went a goal down in the first half, equalized in the second, then had a golden chance to go ahead only a few minutes later when they were awarded a penalty for handball by the England captain, Eddie Hapgood. But Jackie Coulter's kick hit the bar, the Irish lost 2–1, and didn't beat England in England between 1914 and 1957.
- In 1908, in the first match for either country, Sweden conceded a goal to Norway after only 45 seconds – then, with the score still 1–0, became the first team to miss two penalties in a single international, through Karl Gustafsson (saved by Sverre Lie) and Erik Borjesson (shot wide). Gustafsson went on to score twice, Borjesson four times, as Sweden won 11–3!

- Gary Bailey saved three spot kicks for Manchester United at Ipswich in March 1980, from Kevin Beattie (twice taken) and Frans Thijssen. United still lost 6–0!
- Gary Lineker began the 1991–92 football season needing to score 5 goals to break Bobby Charlton's England record of 49. His volley against Poland took England to the European finals, he scored against France and the CIS, and went into the game against Brazil at Wembley needing just one more to match Charlton.

  After only ten minutes, chasing a ball into the right-hand side of the area, he went round the goalkeeper, 36-year-old Carlos Gallo, who may or may not have got a touch to Lineker's head. Scottish referee Jim McClusky gave the penalty.

  Lineker had scored four times from the spot for England, earning each one (etiher by being fouled or forcing a handball), sending the keeper the wrong way each time. He did the same here, but there was more to it than that.

  Lineker had missed from the spot in the League that season, and his last penalty at Wembley, in the 1991 FA Cup Final, had been saved by Mark Crossley. Plus, in the recent League Cup semi-final, also against Forest, he'd suddenly hit a very soft clip into the middle of the net while Crossley dived. It looked unnecessarily cute at best, positively dangerous if the keeper didn't move.

  Carlos obviously hadn't had use of a video of the semi-final. He threw himself to the right as Lineker ran up. Again it was the chip – but this time, perhaps through nerves, Lineker kicked the ground. Carlos, who was already on it, had time to get back up and make an easy save from what ended as a feeble little shot.

  Remarkably, England didn't set up another chance for Lineker all season. He didn't score in any of his last six internationals, was unreasonably substituted in the very last, the decisive European Championship match against Sweden, and missed Charlton's record by a single goal.

- If it's any consolation to him (and it isn't), one of the ways Bobby himself missed out on that 50th goal for England was from the damned spot.

  At Hampden in 1960, after Graham Leggat had given Scotland the lead, Charlton was fouled in the area, got up, and smashed the kick past Frank Haffey, who was winning his first cap. Fifteen minutes from the end, Scotland's captain Bobby Evans handled and the Hungarian referee, Jeno Sranko, who awarded 55 free-kicks during the match, gave another penalty.

  This time Charlton hit it straight at Haffey, who made the save – only for Sranko to order a retake because the ball hadn't been on the spot (so Scotland were penalized for Charlton's error). Surrounded by 129,000 whistles, he drove the third penalty yards wide and held his head in his hands. Scotland escaped with a draw and shared the Home Championship with England and Wales.

  Charlton didn't take another penalty for England (he'd previously been successful with 3 out of 3). As 15 were awarded during the rest of his international career, it's reasonable to suppose that he'd have made the half-century. As it was, the closest he came was by putting the ball in the net against Holland a fraction after the referee had blown for full-time.
- In two consecutive seasons, complete outsiders reached the Amateur Cup Final, each time losing their chance of winning the trophy by missing a penalty.

  In 1967 Skelmersdale United dominated a strong Hendon team in the semi-final but needed a replay to go through. In the Final, they were held to another goalless draw, this time after extra-time, by Enfield. In the very last minute, Skelmersdale were awarded a penalty, but Alan Bermingham's kick was saved by Ian Wolstenholme. Enfield won the replay 3–0.

  Next year, Chesham took the lead but fell behind 2–1 against Leytonstone thanks to a blunder by Dennis Wells.

With ten minutes to go, they were handed a lifeline, but Kenny Kent's penalty was saved.

Skelmersdale won the Cup in 1971. Chesham never did.

- After becoming the first British club to win the European Cup, Celtic had a number of frustrating seasons in the competition, losing the title in the first round the following season, in extra-time after taking the lead in the 1970 Final, and in a bloodstained semi in 1974.

  Having beaten Inter in the 1967 Final, they were eliminated by both Milanese clubs without scoring a goal. In 1969 they drew away from home but were beaten by Pierino Prati's breakaway goal at Parkhead (Milan went on to win the Cup). Three years later they again drew 0–0 in the San Siro, but Inter held out in the return. For the first time, one of the European Cup finalists would be decided by a penalty shoot-out.

  First up for Celtic was substitute John Deans, inevitably nicknamed Dixie, an out-and-out striker and the only player to score a hat-trick in the Final of both the main Scottish Cups. He was certainly out-and-out here, firing the kick over the bar. The other nine went in. Celtic were out and (like Inter) haven't reached the Final since.
- In September 1973, Notts County went to Portsmouth for a Second Division match they tried hard not to win. Kevin Randall missed from a penalty which had to be retaken. Don Masson hit the bar. Another retake. This time Brian Stubbs had his shot saved. Not many teams can have used three players to miss the same penalty three times. County, nevertheless, won 2–1.
- In a 1978 World Cup with no outstanding team, Scotland had as good a chance as anyone, so much so that you could even agree with manager Ally McLeod's trumpetings, especially after the forceful win over Czechoslovakia in the qualifiers. The third match in the finals, against Holland, would decide who topped the group, said loud McLeod, but

qualification itself was a formality: only Peru and Iran stood in the way.

McLeod's confidence seemed to be based on the assumption that Peruvians don't like it up 'em, that Teofilo Cubillas, the star winger from 1970, was overweight and superannuated, and the goalkeeper a madman who didn't like crosses.

In fact, Cubillas was only 29, younger than either Bruce Rioch or Don Masson, the Derby midfield pairing McLeod was still relying on even though they'd been in obvious decline all season. Up front, Munante and Oblitas were the fastest wingers in South America, faced by a rookie full-back (Stuart Kennedy) and another playing out of position (Martin Buchan). McLeod's homework really was of the 'see me' variety. As for the goalkeeper, he didn't have many crosses to deal with.

Soon after Jordan had put Scotland ahead in the 15th minute, the writing was on the wall. During half-time, with the scores level and Cubillas beginning to run things, it's said that the limit of McLeod's tactical instruction was to tell the goalkeeper Allan Rough to kick the ball harder to clear the Peruvian midfield! In the second half, more of the same: Scotland hanging on, Oblitas robbing Rioch to make a headed chance for La Rosa.

Then, on the hour, against a run of play, help was at hand. Swedish referee Ulf Eriksson decided that Cubillas had brought down Rioch in the area, and Don Masson stepped up for the kick.

In the final qualifying match against Wales at Anfield, Masson's penalty, awarded for a handball by Jones, had sent Scotland to Argentina. Now, as then, he hit the ball to his left, but this time the goalkeeper didn't go the wrong way. The kick was soft and at a comfortable height, and Ramon Quiroga, who revelled in being as crazy as they said, pushed it away.

Two sweet long shots by Cubillas won the match for Peru, Scotland could only draw with Iran, and went out despite a win over the Dutch that showed what might have been. It was the last time big things were expected of them in the World Cup. Masson, substituted by Archie Gemmill twenty minutes from time, didn't win another cap.

- In 1988, penalties were missed in both the major English Cup Finals as well as the European Championship Final and the Finals of two of the European club Cups.

In the League Cup, holders Arsenal trailed the underdogs Luton at half-time before recovering through Martin Hayes and Alan Smith then earning a penalty, which seemed certain to put them 3–1 ahead. But Andy Dibble, who'd been at fault with Smith's cross–shot, saved Nigel Winterburn's kick, Danny Wilson equalized, and Brian Stein scored his second goal. Luton won 3–2 and reached the Final the following year.

In the FA Cup Final, Liverpool were overwhelming favourites, the acquisition of John Barnes and Peter Beardsley turning them from an awesome side into one touched by brilliance. Tom Finney regarded their recent 5–0 win over Forest as the best team performance he'd ever seen.

Still, if any team could be guaranteed at least to make things difficult for them, it was aggressive, niggly, up-and-under Wimbledon, a non-League club only eleven years earlier, now the underdogs not many wanted to see win, a team built round the fouls of Vincent Peter Jones and elbows of Fash the Bash. Gazza, among others, hadn't escaped Vinny's clutches for long.

In the Final, after Lawrie Sanchez had headed them in front, Wimbledon frustrated Liverpool at every turn, paying Beardsley their own brand of attention, closing Barnes right down. Then, against the run of things, Liverpool were awarded a penalty of doubtful provenance.

When Ian Rush went off for his unhappy year in Turin, Liverpool were expected to struggle for goals. In came John Aldridge, Rush lookalike and natural striker with Oxford United (and later Tranmere). He finished the season as First Division leading scorer with 26 goals, and put away two more in the semi-final, the first from a penalty.

Now he ran up to knock in the equalizer that would probably turn the match. Wimbledon's captain Dave Beasant dived to his left with complete confidence and pushed the ball away: the first penalty miss in an FA Cup Final at Wembley.

The following year, Aldridge scored the first goal of the Final (his substitute, I. Rush, scored the other two) as Liverpool won the Cup. But for his penalty miss and Michael Thomas' last-minute goal at Anfield in 1989, the club would have won two Doubles in a row.

In Stuttgart, favourites PSV Eindhoven played below form against a very defensive Benfica. Result: the second European Cup Final to be decided on penalties after a goalless draw.

The first eleven kicks went in. The twelfth, by full-back Antonio Veloso, was saved by Hans Van Breukelen. Benfica, who lost again in the 1990 Final, haven't won the Cup since 1962.

Although Holland had lost to the USSR in their first group match, they were expected to win the European Championship Final. Their class players were on form: the captain, Ruud Gullit, 37-year-old Arnold Muhren wide on the left, Frank Rijkaard and Ronald Koeman at the back; above all, Marco Van Basten, who'd scored the first hat-trick against England for twenty-nine years and the last-minute winner in the semi-final. There'd also been some luck: Hoddle and Lineker hitting the woodwork with the score still 0–0, Wim Kieft scoring a freak goal eight minutes from time to squeeze out the Republic of Ireland.

The USSR had some fine players too – Demyanenko, Rats, Zavarov, Dassaev, Mikhailichenko – but the suspension of Oleg Kiznetsov left a weakness in the centre of their defence.

Holland exploited it to lead 2–0 after 53 minutes, Gullit heading in Van Basten's headed pass, the latter finishing Muhren's long cross with an unbelievable volley over Dassaev from a narrow angle, the kind of inspiration the USSR didn't have.

Nevertheless they kept trying. On the hour, Van Breukelen brought down Sergei Gotsmanov when he didn't have to, and Igor Belanov ran from the edge of the semi-circle to hit the penalty.

European Footballer of the Year in 1986 on the strength of a single run and shot (admittedly a stunning goal against Belgium in the World Cup), the slight, balding Belanov had scored a hat-trick against the Belgians, including a penalty, but had been used largely as a substitute since 1987 and was in no great form now. His long run did more to upset his rhythm than terrify Van Breukelen, who made up for his hasty foul by saving with his knees. Holland, never under threat again, coasted home 2–0. Van Breukelen's penalty saves had won the European Cup and European Championship within a month.

Finally, in the UEFA Cup Final, Bayer Leverkusen produced one of the great European comebacks. Trailing 3–0 from the first leg against Español, they were held goalless at half-time and seemed to have no chance.

Then the Brazilian Tita scored after 56 minutes, the East German Falko Gotz made it 2–0, and the Korean Cha Bum Kun 3–0 with nine minutes left. There were no goals in extra-time. See Chapter 5 for details of the shoot-out.

- Wales, needing to beat Romania in Cardiff to qualify for the 1994 World Cup finals, fell behind when Neville Southall fumbled Gheorghe Hagi's long shot, were outclassed in every department, but hit a purple patch on the hour, Dean

Saunders equalizing from close range, Gary Speed winning a penalty very soon afterwards.

It looked as if this wasn't to be Dan Petrescu's day. Earlier, he'd hit a post in front of an open goal. Now he was judged to have brought Speed down, and Paul Bodin stepped up to take the penalty that would probably win the match.

Bodin's left foot had scored three goals for Wales, all from the spot. He'd never missed an international penalty. He struck this one firmly past Florin Prunea's right hand – and hit the bar.

It was the start of a depressing night for the Welsh: Florin Raducioiu's winner sent Romania through; Southall, Rush and Hughes lost probably their last chance of playing in the finals; Terry Yorath wasn't retained as manager; a spectator was killed by a firework after the final whistle.

Three days later, Bodin's successful penalty earned a point in Swindon's relegation battle.

• After losing their opening match in the 1978 World Cup qualifiers (2–0 in Prague; Andy Gray sent off), Scotland needed a little luck. They got it when Ian Evans' own goal gave them a 1–0 win over Wales at Hampden. They then beat Czechoslovakia in the return, and went into the last match, against Wales, needing only a draw to qualify.

Moving the game to Anfield turned a home match for Wales into a Scottish sing-along. Already without Leighton James, the Welsh were forced back from the start, Dai Davies making a fine save from Dalglish. Somehow they held on, had a chance to go ahead through Peter Sayer, and looked the better side up to half-time and beyond, forcing Allan Rough to a fingertip save on the hour.

Soon afterwards, Willie Johnston put a long throw-in into the area, a group of players went up for it, one of them used a hand. French referee Robert Wurtz gave a penalty against David Jones. Television replays fingered Joe Jordan.

Don Masson sent Davies the wrong way from the spot,

Dalglish headed a second, Scotland went to the finals, Wales haven't reached them since 1958. In 1982 Jordan became the only British player to score in the final stages of three World Cups. In 1981, a few years too late, he was sent off against Wales.

The goal that sent Scotland to the 1986 finals, again at Wales' expense, was also scored from the penalty spot.

- The Arsenal that Herbert Chapman built dominated the 1930s, winning five League Championships and two FA Cups, providing a record seven players for a single England team. In 1932–33 they scored more goals than any other club in the country (118) in winning the first of three consecutive Division One titles. On 14 January they appeared at Fellows Park in the third round of the FA Cup.

While Chapman was spending record sums to build his squads, the town of Walsall was suffering the worst of the Depression. A 'Spending for Employment' campaign was set up: whatever you can spare – to have a coat mended, say, or a door repaired, anything – spend it to provide local people with work. Only 11,149 could afford to watch the Arsenal match.

Walsall the team hadn't won away all season. Although unbeaten at home, they lay 54 places below Arsenal in the League, 10th in the Third Division North – and Chapman decided it was safe enough to do a little experimenting.

Out went a string of first choices: Bob John, Eddie Hapgood, Joe Hulme, Jack Lambert. In came Norman Sidey and Tommy Black in defence, Billy Warnes and Charlie Walsh up front. Of the four, only Sidey had any first-team experience – but Walsh, at least, wasn't lacking in confidence: he thought himself the best centre-forward at the club. He spread the word that he was about to play the game of his life.

He did. He missed at least four clear-cut chances, including a perfect cross from Cliff Bastin that hit him on the shoulder, and a pass that was on its way to the unmarked David Jack before he got in the way. After a goalless first half, Chapman moved him aside and put Jack at centre-forward, but the tide was already moving one way.

Walsall, on a win bonus of £5 a man (average wage £6), had sailed into Arsenal from the start, cutting Herbie Roberts' eye, fouling Bastin and Alex James. On the hour, Fred Lee's cross was headed in by Gilbert Alsop, who was then fouled in the penalty area by Black (another new boy having a bad one). Bill Sheppard's penalty sealed one of the biggest Cup upsets imaginable.

Arsenal's seven internationals (Bastin, James and Jack were among the best of all time) lived to play another day. So too did Sidey (just). But Black was transferred to Plymouth within a week; Walsh to Brentford within a month; Warnes to Norwich at the end of the season.

- The goalkeeper who played for Australia against a touring English FA eleven in 1951 probably cursed his parents' sense of humour all his life, never more so than after the second international, which Australia lost 17–0.

  The goalkeeper's surname was Conquest. His parents must have thought it a real wheeze when they christened him Norman. After the match, the headlines wrote themselves.
- If ever a club's name seemed to be engraved on the FA Cup, it was Nottingham Forest's in 1990–91. After Tony Gale was controversially sent off in the semi-final, West Ham were overrun 4–0. When Gazza wrecked his knee in the Final, Stuart Pearce scored from the free-kick; then Mark Crossley saved a penalty from Lineker, who also had a goal wrongly disallowed. After a lifetime's disappointment in the FA Cup, this looked just the ticket for Cloughie.

  But there was an ironic slip 'twixt Cup and lip. After Paul Stewart's second-half goal had forced extra-time, Des Walker went up at the far post, got there first, and headed into his own net: Clough's last chance ended by a mistake from the best defender in the country. Tottenham won the Cup for a record eighth time, Forest lost in the Final for the first. They haven't won it since 1959.

- Penalty shoot-outs apart, Argentina scored only two goals in their last four matches of Italia '90, both by the electric blond-haired Claudio Caniggia, whose glancing header equalized in the semi-final against the hosts in Naples.

  Argentina held on to win on penalties, as they'd done in the quarter-final – but Caniggia, who seemed to have some kind of death wish, had tried to handle the ball more than once as it went over his head. Why, nobody knows. Eight minutes from the end he'd finally reached it, whereupon Michel Vautrot booked him for deliberate handball.

  It was his second caution of the tournament and he had to miss the Final. Argentina, hit by injuries, and an average team even at their best, never looked like scoring without him, massed in defence, and lost to a contentious late penalty.

- Denmark, in the World Cup finals for the first time, had more world-class footballers than any other team in 1986: captain and sweeper Morten Olsen; Frank Arnesen and Soren Lerby in midfield; the strong-running Proben Elkjaer up front with Michael Laudrup, who looked like becoming one of the greats. So much quality that Jan Molby and Jesper Olsen, both with English clubs, were used mainly as substitutes.

  The Danes won all three matches in the hardest of the six groups, beating Scotland and West Germany without conceding a goal, thrashing the fancied Uruguayans 6–1.

  In the second-round match against Spain, for a place in the quarter-finals, Klaus Berggreen was tripped by Gallego in the area, Jesper Olsen sent Zubizarreta the wrong way from the penalty spot, and Denmark were on the march again.

  Two minutes from half-time, the same Olsen dropped back and out to the right to pick up a short ball from keeper

Lars Hogh, rolled it around to kill a little time, then knocked it back to the keeper without really looking up. It didn't get there. Butragueño, lurking with no real intent, received it on a plate, and slipped it past Hogh without breaking stride.

The blunder cut into Denmark's confidence. Twelve minutes after half-time, Butragueño was left unmarked to head a second. Ten minutes after that, he was brought down by Soren Busk, and Goicoechea put away the penalty. Butragueño scored two more, one a penalty, to equal the World Cup finals record; Spain won 5–1.

The Danes walked off, the shell-shock evident in Elkjaer's TV interview. Denmark won the 1992 European Championship, against expectations, but have never had a team like this, before or since.

Appendix 2

PENALTY SHOOT-OUT QUESTIONNAIRE

Please provide brief answers to the questions below, either on the sheet itself in the spaces provided, or on a separate sheet of paper. An envelope is enclosed for your reply. Thank you for your co-operation.

1. Would you abolish the penalty shoot-out as a method of resolving drawn matches, and if so, why?

I WOULD KEEP THEM

2. If you like penalty shoot-outs, please provide reasons why.

IT IS EXCITING
& NERVE RACKING
AND I DON'T SEE WHY
THE SYSTEM SHOULD CHANGE.

GOOD LUCK WITH YOUR BOOK

3. If you would abolish the shoot-out, what would you put in its place and why? Please select one option from the list below and add some brief reasons for your choice:

- **The Golden Goal** – sudden-death extra-time, where the first team to score wins the match. It should be noted that this is FIFA's current preference.
- **USA-style 'one-on-one' shoot-out** – the penalty taker starts 35 yards from goal and has five seconds to beat the goalkeeper.
- **Corners** – the team awarded the most corners during regulation and extra-time wins.
- **Possession** – the team which has the most possession wins.
- **Attacking possession** – the team which has the most possession in the opponents' half of the field is awarded the match.
- **Disappearing players** – a phased reduction in the number of players on the pitch during extra-time. At regular intervals each team loses a player in an attempt to increase the chances of a deciding goal.
- **A penalty shoot-out before extra-time** – the result of the shoot-out is used to decide the winner in the event the match is still drawn after extra-time.
- **The first goal in extra-time counts double** – in the event there is still a draw after extra-time the team scoring first wins. If no goals are scored then it's back to penalties.
- **Tossing a coin or drawing lots from a hat.**
- **Replays** – replay the match until there is a result.

Please feel free to add any comments you might have on any of these options, each of which has been put forward at some time or another as an alternative to the shoot-out.

J.D.C. Miller – September 1997

6

Acknowledgements

I know from the many letters I have received following Clark's death that his book has stimulated great interest and not a little controversy. On reading through his manuscript and files I realized that he received encouragement and support from many sources. I now owe these individuals and their organizations a great debt. They were all, without exception, courteous and helpful to my son, and did all they could to further his research.

So, I'd like to thank, in particular: Gerhard Aigner and Fritz Ahlstrom from UEFA, William Campbell of the Irish Football Association, Francis Lee, Ken Ridden the FA Director of Refereeing, and Mr David Barber at the FA library, Eric Walker, Chairman of the Scottish Football Independent Review Commission, Dr M. Williams of the Human Sciences Department at Liverpool University, Mr D.H. Wills, FIFA Vice President, Keith Cooper, FIFA Director of Communications, and Maurice Schneider from the FIFA Communications Division. And, finally, a special and warm thanks to Ian Preece, Clark's editor at Victor Gollancz, who was very helpful and supportive over the last hurdle, gently guiding me through the final stages.

James Miller

Acknowledgements